Disciple-Making Culture gives standing of the biblical mandate to make disciples but also the knowledge of *how to create a culture that encourages discipleship* in our ministries or churches. Author Brandon Guindon brilliantly shows us how to develop disciples in a way that says "you can do it," and that others can too. We all need to get better at discipleship, and this book will help you and your church do just that!

— **Dave Ferguson**, Author of *Hero Maker*

This book bears the seed of a movement. Systems and strategies cannot beget culture. Culture is born from a wedding of intentional purpose and sometimes painful experiences. Brandon weaves these together in a biblical way that focuses on highly relational factors. The result is an infinitely reproducible culture.

— **Ralph Moore**, Hope Chapel Founder, Author of *Making Disciples*

In the twenty years I've known Brandon, he has served as a volunteer discipleship leader in our church and a staff leader of our small groups ministry. With the Lord's help, he grew that ministry from twelve to 600 groups. When Brandon became Executive Pastor, he helped us establish relational discipleship as the foundation of everything we do as a church. I see how God is using him, now a church planter and coach to other church leaders, to create a relational disciple-making culture wherever he goes. If you want to grow in your understanding of a disciple-making culture, you need to read this book.

— **Jim Putman**, Lead Pastor, Real Life Ministries in Post Falls, Idaho

This book is my new go-to book when I recommend resources to church leaders who want to create a disciple-making culture. Every church leader should read it.

— **Bobby Harrington**, Point Leader for Discipleship.org and Renew.org

God has used Brandon over the last few years to coach the church I serve as we embrace a seismic shift in our culture. On our transformational journey toward creating a disciple-making culture, Brandon has loved us, helped us, grieved with us, celebrated with us, and, most importantly, discipled us—using the very concepts he writes about in this book. Pastors, church planters, elders, staff members, and small group facilitators should read this book with their teams. It is profoundly Christ-centered, yet amazingly simple. Your application of this book will change the trajectory of your church as it has changed the trajectory of ours.

— **David Garison**, Lead Pastor, Northside Christian Church in Spring, Texas

BRANDON GUINDON

DISCIPLE MAKING CULTURE

*Cultivate Thriving Disciple-Makers
Throughout Your Church*

Foreword by Bill Hull

A **DISCIPLESHIP.ORG** RESOURCE

Disciple-Making Culture: Cultivate Thriving Disciple-Makers Throughout Your Church
Copyright © 2020 by Brandon Guindon

To my grandparents, Bob and Bonnie Guindon.
Both of you have played a huge role in my life. Grandma, you have
always inspired me to be kind to others and see the best in people.
Much of my passion for developing others comes from your investment
in my life. Gramps, your ability to tell stories and your love of life
have greatly influenced me. It's no surprise I too love to motivate
others through story.

Thank you both, and I love you.

CONTENTS

ACKNOWLEDGEMENTS

A special thanks to my great friend and co-laborer in writing this book and almost all of my writing projects, Lisa Malstrom. I appreciate your gifting, wisdom, and encouragement throughout the writing of this book.

Thank you to my friend Darrell Roquemore. Your perspective and advice improved this book.

Thank you to Troy Hawks and Joel Owen, two of my close pastor friends who contributed to the content of this book. You are both living out disciple-making culture in your lives and your churches. Keep pressing on in this journey.

Finally, thank you to all my elders and staff members. Each of you has done an incredible job establishing, sustaining, and protecting our church culture so that it, which is based on the actions and teachings of Jesus, is now a model for others. I appreciate each of you, and I am thankful to Jesus for how he has used you to build a disciple-making culture at Real Life Ministries Texas.

FOREWORD

It's common for us in the church to be so passionate about what we say, yet so passive in what we do. We are experts at making our purpose and work sound revolutionary, but we often live complacent and satisfied lives. In this environment, you can be labeled a radical by sitting in a different pew on Sunday, or by altering your parking spot or the service you attend. Possibly you go out on a limb and suggest the worship team lower the decibels or use a little less of the smoke machine. You can cause everyone to "man their battle stations" by challenging the song selection or suggesting they sing fewer songs that make knowing God sound like he's part of a teen romance. In many ways, we have reduced ourselves to a pretend world. When we are in church, we merely imagine heroic things, like Jesus challenging the religious establishment and taking on the Roman Empire, or the apostle Paul going to jail and being shipwrecked, beaten, and left for dead outside of cities. We are inspired by these stories and we're so glad they did these things for us so that now we can enjoy the good lives we have. Frankly, we too often encounter no more trouble in society than our non-believing neighbors do.

Our problems and challenges are restricted to the fact that we are humans, inhabitants of the first world, but there are no challenges in our lives that come to us because we are distinctly Christian. This is because we try—dare I say pretend—to do something radical and meaningful, but we don't hold ourselves accountable to actually do what Jesus told us to do—*make disciples of all nations.* Because if we did hold ourselves to that, we would soon find out there was nothing pretend about all those biblical stories. We would be living into those stories. Those heroic acts would be our acts, those troubles would be our troubles, and those great accomplishments would be our accomplishments.

I will tell you what takes courage: to reverse engineer the Great Commission and apply it to your life and ministry. Are you ready to do that? Start by answering the following questions honestly, using Matthew 28:18–20 as your basis for answers:

- Can you define what a disciple is?
- Can you describe how to make disciples?
- Have you made any new disciples? How do you know if you have done this?
- When Jesus said, "Make disciples of *all nations*," he meant we need to make many new disciples. Have you made *many* new disciples?
- Have you made many new disciples who are eighteen years of age and older, who are not children of congregants?
- How many of these disciples are now well-taught and mature?
- Have you been involved in all of this yourself?

I know this for sure: if you ask these questions to your church leaders, point blank, it will create organizational havoc, scrutiny, and pushback. The questions I listed above threaten the entire pretend world of cosmetic religion. The reason I wrote the foreword to this book is because it offers a practical way to stop pretending, to face up to the questions I have asked, and to actually build a disciple-making ministry that will revolutionize your life and your church.

Brandon offers in this book four components of a culture that can create more than just a church: they create an actual disciple-making movement within your church. He is able to not only write about it but he is also living it in community with a growing congregation. I have met many of his leaders; they are infectiously enthusiastic, loving, ordinary people with a sense of mission and power. I love being around them—it is obvious to me that God is present among them, because God promised to be with all of us when we get on the same page with him.

Remember what Jesus promised disciple-makers: "I am with you always, even to the end." That is not a throwaway line or a promise given to just anyone; it is reserved for those who are intentionally giving their lives to making disciples.

Read this, yes, but Brandon won't allow you to simply get away with that. Once you start reading it, you will find yourself compelled to act on it.

—**Bill Hull**, author of *The Disciple-Making Church* and co-author of *The Discipleship Gospel*

INTRODUCTION

W hy write a book about disciple-making culture? My answer starts when God called me into full-time ministry almost twenty years ago. I had the opportunity to be part of an incredible movement of God at Real Life Ministries in Post Falls, Idaho, led by Jim Putman and the rest of the team. I mention Jim here because he led the church plant that provided the first disciple-making culture I ever experienced. We followed God on an incredible journey—one that continues to this day—where thousands of people have come to Christ and are being discipled. As a result, we impacted an entire community. We watched the Holy Spirit begin a movement of disciple-making that continues to plant churches, impact pastors, and inspire leaders all over the globe.

Fifteen years after joining Real Life Ministries in Idaho, my wife and I planted a church in Tomball, Texas (just north of Houston). As we prepared to plant, I wondered if the miracle that happened in Post Falls could be reproduced in a church plant in Texas. Was that an isolated event that God did in the Pacific Northwest? So often during my time at Real Life Ministries in Idaho, I had heard other pastors say to me, "What happened in Post Falls was just a freak thing."

But was it unique to that location? I really sat back and thought about this question. Everything in me rebelled against that notion, but I had to find out for myself. I knew that God calls all of us to go and make disciples, but I didn't see that happening. So rather than view what happened in my early years of ministry as a miracle,

I thought, *Shouldn't we view it as the norm?* As a result, we took the plunge and planted a church in Texas.

Because of my previous experiences, our new church plant was committed to building a disciple-making culture from day one. This meant that we sought to live out the Great Commission as if it had been imprinted in our DNA. Taking all the principles I had learned in Scripture and the practical lessons I learned at Real Life Ministries in Post Falls, Idaho, we launched Real Life Ministries Texas.

What I discovered in making the transition from Idaho to Texas was the critical necessity of establishing a disciple-making culture. I'm writing this book to pass on to you the hope, ideas, and practical tools I have learned that can help you transform the culture of your church into a disciple-making culture. No matter what stage your church is in—whether brand new or very old—it carries within it the potential, by the power of the Holy Spirit, to become something new.

> *Your church carries within it the potential to become something new.*

Planting Real Life Ministries Texas

Our church started out as a small group meeting in my back yard, but we quickly began to grow. Now, after three years, our weekly attendance is over 800 people and growing every week. We believe that fulfilling the Great Commission is not an impossible task or a rare once-in-a-lifetime miracle. It's a regular, everyday journey that we all can join. But it's more than just a journey: it's a commitment to *being* something rather than merely *doing* something. Fulfilling the Great Commission is about cultivating a culture of disciple-making, where following Jesus is our natural practice, not just something we do through a program. Those who participate in a culture like this understand that they are disciples who make disciples—and they know how to do it. It's a culture that calls people to live a lifestyle rather than merely participate in a program. This culture sets us on a journey that reaches back in time and connects us to the culture Jesus modeled and the early church lived out, where lives are changed. The journey produces compelling stories that people want to hear and a compelling community that people want to join.

Church leaders who know about the miracles we have seen ask me questions about the mechanics of what we do. Yet I often sense they are asking a deeper question—a soul-gnawing, heart-gripping question—under the guise of their questions about curriculum and small group structure. I sense in them a desire to know how to cultivate a culture at their church where the kind of relationships exist in which true biblical disciple-making could occur. When I have sat and talked with thousands of pastors and other Christians, I see in their eyes a deep longing to be a disciple who knows how to make disciples.

That, my friends, is why I am writing this book—to answer the question that plagues our hearts when we look at the Great Commission: How do we actually live this out? It's not just about how *I* live this out *as an individual*, but how *we* create a culture of disciple-making *as a church*, where being disciples who make disciples is who we are. I hope to inspire you to build a culture like this.

When I write about "culture," I don't mean the culture of society as a whole. I'm writing about culture in churches and I use the term "culture" in this book to mean *the way a church naturally functions when they are not under pressure*. Culture is not what happens in a simulated experience or in a classroom, where people can provide the right answers when prompted; culture is what happens naturally *as the way things normally go*. In business, people talk about company "culture," which is the general atmosphere of how a company operates, especially when it comes to the attitudes and habits of the employees. Since we're talking about church culture, though, perhaps the simplest way to describe the kind of culture I want to help you create is to say an "early church" culture. Jesus' way of life transformed his followers and affected the culture of the first church. That's what I'm getting at here, and that's what I seek to help you find and cultivate in your church context.

Discipleship vs. Disciple-Making

The heat of Africa can sometimes surpass even Houston's warmth, and on one particular day during a teaching trip I took to the African country of Ethiopia, the heat in the classroom was stifling. I stood in front of a room of Ethiopian church planters, who stared back at me with confused looks on their faces. I had already spent the better part of the day training this group of leaders on Jesus' methods for disciple-making as outlined in Scripture. I began describing both the life of a disciple and what it looks like to make disciples, but I stopped talking when I realized that something must have been lost in translation.

Wiping sweat from my brow, I turned to my translator and asked, "What am I saying that is creating confusion?"

He said, "I think you need to answer an important question: What is the difference between discipleship and disciple-making?"

I realized that I had been using these terms, and the word "disciple," without clarifying my definitions for each of them. When speaking through the translator, the problem became even more glaring due to language differences. It was more than just a translation issue, though; I have learned that there is a vital distinction between these terms in English too. In the Western church we confuse these terms, and our past experiences may cloud our understanding of them. Let me tell you what I learned as a result of this experience.

First, in order for us to really rediscover the meaning of these key terms, we must be aware of *different perspectives*. When I was speaking to my Ethiopian brothers, I continued to mix perspectives.

I spoke about characteristics of a disciple alongside my description of the roles and responsibilities of a disciple-maker. This caused confusion. The truth is that a follower of Jesus can grow as a disciple yet never become a disciple-maker. So I found it helpful to say that the process of growing spiritually as a disciple is called discipleship, which does not necessarily include disciple-making for all people depending on where they are on their journey.

Second, church leaders must understand and be committed to their mission of making disciples who make disciples. Creating a disciple-making culture will require you to discover what Jesus did through his actions and lifestyle as he built a culture for his followers. Those he discipled in that culture became not just disciples, but world-changing disciple-makers. When I understood my mishap with the translator, I began to separate the concepts and distinctly define the terms in this way: discipleship is the process of growth for the one being discipled, and disciple-making is the process that disciple-makers engage in when they invest into the lives of those God calls them to disciple.

In light of these definitions, I invite you, as you read this book, to be aware of different perspectives around you, be committed to the core mission of the church, and answer hard questions. These questions may challenge you, like, "How do we cultivate a culture like Jesus and the early church, where disciples lived out radical spiritual growth?" and, "What occurs when a group of people have a fearless pursuit of the Great Commission and a strong sense of urgency?" I will warn you, though, answering questions like these is not for the faint of heart. And remember the Great Commission comes with both a promise and a warning label: Jesus will be with us, yet following him might cost us everything. My hope is that as you read this book, the pages of Scripture will become more real to you and the examples I describe—of success and of failure—motivate you to "go" as Jesus commanded. When you do this, these stories become not just something you read about, but real life experiences—like what happened with my friend Greg.

A Real Life Story

I met Greg in the aftermath of Hurricane Harvey. This disaster devastated the Houston Area, but at the same time, it was one of the greatest blessings to me because, in the muddy mess of the flood, I met Greg and his family. Harvey camped over South Texas for nearly a week in August 2017. You may recall watching on the news Houstonians boating down flooded roads and through swamped neighborhoods. It wasn't staged footage—it was all too real. Fifty-four inches of rain fell on the Houston Area within forty-eight hours. Our little church plant had purchased some buildings north of Houston and, until the hurricane, we had been spending every possible moment renovating the space so that we could launch church services in our new location. When the hurricane hit, we were fortunate that our buildings and the immediate area around them were mostly spared from flood damage, but neighborhoods all around us were literally under water.

We quickly shifted our focus from renovating our building to assembling small teams of people from our church to go out and help families who were impacted by the flooding. From a makeshift control center in our partially finished building, we assigned teams to go into neighborhoods we knew had sustained damage. Armed with heavy-duty cleaning supplies and plastic bags, our teams waded down flooded streets to offer assistance. I was on a team with three others, and the first house my team arrived at belonged to a family of five: Greg, Laura, and their three daughters. They were sorting through the belongings that could be salvaged and were more than happy for us to help them start the process of recovery. Greg and Laura had been away from church much of their married lives, and Greg wanted nothing to do with it. He was, however, open to spending time with a group of guys outside of church.

Several times a month, I invite men over to my house and we sit in the back yard and just talk about life. Three weeks after Harvey, I invited my new friend Greg to come hang out with a group of guys. He showed up, and our friendship began. Even though Greg is from South Africa and was raised in a different culture, he and I had a great deal in common. As the months went by, Greg continued to come over. Then one Sunday morning, he led his family through the doors of our church. Greg remained cautious and skeptical, but he was willing to continue to meet with me and spend time together. I kept inviting him to the small group that my wife, Amber, and I were leading in our home, and he and Laura eventually came.

Over the months and years since Hurricane Harvey hit, Greg has grown spiritually in leaps and bounds. That December, just six months after we met, Greg was baptized, and then he baptized his wife and three daughters the same day. Greg and his entire family were growing rapidly in their walk with Christ. In the months that followed, Greg and I continued to live life together as we met in small group, and on multiple occasions, Greg even led our small group.

One of the greatest moments in my twenty years of ministry happened just one year after Greg's baptism. He stood up at our men's monthly breakfast at church, which had over sixty guys in attendance, and taught the devotional lesson. He did a magnificent job! Not only is Greg now discipling people in small group, he is also beginning to use the gifts God has given him to influence the men in our church.

So how did this happen? How did Greg go from a non-believing, anti-church guy to someone who passionately and intentionally disciples others? What happened in and around his life in eighteen short months that led him to stand in front of the men of our church to speak about the power of disciple-making?

God worked through the culture of our church to impact Greg's life. Our culture, like any culture, is simply "the way we do things." But disciple-making culture in a church is intentionally created, lived out, and passed on to people in a local body of believers. Church culture is not the product of what is merely written on a church bulletin or declared in a set of by-laws; it's the product of the deep values and convictions of those who live within the culture.

Why Is Church Culture Important?

Peter Drucker, the Austrian-born American management consultant and author who has greatly influenced modern business practices, is credited with the popular maxim, "Culture eats strategy for breakfast." I often see churches try to implement the newest strategies or reinvent the programs of other churches. While we can try to impart all kinds of strategies and programs, we need to first consider our *church culture* because people always gravitate back to "who we are." In our church we often say of disciple-making, "It's not what we do; it's who we are." But many churches are simply not disciple-making churches, which is a culture issue, not just a strategy issue. Strategy won't make a lasting impact if disciple-making is not "who we are."

Culture is created through consistent behavior over time, a lifestyle of living out core values that govern our actions. Chasing different strategies without a clear disciple-making culture will cause leaders to implement strategies that are unsustainable, doomed to fail, or, at best, mildly effective. Without a clear vision and a well-established culture, these leaders will constantly shift their culture, leaving their church community confused and disillusioned.

Recently, I was speaking to a group of pastors about how to cultivate a healthy disciple-making culture in their churches. During one of the breaks, a pastor came up to me and asked, "What curriculum do you use for your discipling program?" I could see that he was putting the cart before the horse, though, so I answered him with another question: "Whom are you currently discipling?"

He looked away, and I could see his face flushed with embarrassment. He turned back to me with tears in his eyes and said, "Brother, I've been in ministry almost forty years, and I can honestly say I have never been discipled, and I am not sure if I have ever intentionally discipled anyone other than maybe my kids."

This interaction illustrates why cultivating a disciple-making culture is so important. The pastor wanted a strategy, but culture doesn't develop from a strategy. It's the other way around: strategies come from culture, whether it is a healthy or an unhealthy culture. Unhealthy church culture, at best, leads to ineffective churches, but more alarmingly, it has the potential to harm individuals and the reputation of Jesus. So how can you create a healthy disciple-making culture in your church? I commend to you four key components to help you transition your church toward embracing a culture of disciple-making.

The Four Key Components of a Disciple-Making Culture

During my years working with Real Life Ministries in Idaho, we identified the key components of disciple-making. In *Real-Life Discipleship Training Manual*, which I co-authored with Jim Putman, Avery Willis, and Bill Krause, we took a practical look at how to live out these components as disciple-makers. In this book, I will build off of the basic ideas of those components and examine how they create and impact a disciple-making culture. This gives us the opportunity to dissect at a deeper level their implications for churches or ministries when their leaders live out and impart these components to others.

First, we must start with the *biblical foundation* of disciple-making culture. We will look and see what examples the Bible reveals for creating and maintaining disciple-making culture in the earliest days of Christianity. What did disciple-making culture look like for Jesus and his disciples? What did it look like in the early church? Jesus is our model, and we do not have the right to substitute his model for any other methods of disciple-making. We have an obligation to look and see what methods Jesus used. *He is the model!*

Because of what I had learned about the biblical foundation of disciple-making, I knew it was important to spend time with Greg because Jesus spent his time with his disciples and potential disciples. That's why I invited Greg to my back yard, because Jesus spent time with people like Zacchaeus, who was a potential disciple of Jesus, as was Greg. It's really that simple. Greg had no interest in a church service; he simply needed relationships. Inviting Greg into a culture focused on discipleship was the first step I took to disciple him. The biblical foundation is not just *what to teach* (Jesus' message) or *who Jesus was* (his identity) but also *Jesus' way of living* (his method). To cultivate a healthy disciple-making culture, we must build upon the biblical foundation that Jesus gives us through his teaching and his lifestyle.

Second, we must understand the important role of *intentional leadership.* Purposeful and deliberate investment in others and in culture itself must happen in order for us to create effective disciples. Intentional disciple-makers know how to make disciples and create a culture of disciple-making. As the leader goes, so goes the culture. When intentionality is lacking, then a culture wanders and becomes a victim of whatever the current trend happens to be. Every church has a culture, whether or not it is intentionally developed. Being intentional includes investing into the lives of new people. That's how Jesus lived: he did nothing by accident because he knew exactly what he wanted to accomplish. He both intentionally

As the leader
goes, so goes
the culture.

invested into those he discipled and created a culture with great purpose so others could invest like he did. Jesus wanted disciples who could make disciples and build a culture of other intentional leaders. We must intentionally live the life of a disciple-maker, and that comes from having leaders *who see their identity as an intentional disciple-maker.*

Third, intentional leaders must create *relational environments.* God created every person with a deep need for connection. We were meant to be in community together, and there is something very powerful when the church gathers corporately and in smaller groups. Our relational need goes beyond just friendship; we long for meaningful connection. We are made in the image of God, and our ability to express the highest human ethic, which is love, cannot happen unless we are in relationship with others. This goes beyond just "hanging out" and involves creating an environment where we are learning to apply biblical truth and grow in our love for God and others. The relational environment is guided by intentional leadership toward a specific purpose, which is the reproducible process.

Finally, we come to the necessity of a *reproducible process.* A reproducible process of disciple-making is when the people of a church can effectively replicate what they have learned. When an intentional leader consistently communicates the culture I've described in this book in a way that is simple to understand, moves people toward mission, and is joyful to live out, people will celebrate and repeat the behaviors that define that culture. Then, it is possible for this type of culture to be passed down through generations, replicated in other churches, and even adopted into the culture of individual families.

Greg's life was forever changed because he experienced a culture built upon these components. His life proclaimed the evidence that he was a disciple of Jesus. Due to the intentional investment from me and other disciples around him, a culture of disciple-making gave him a model for disciple-making, and he grew in the owner-ship of his faith. A powerful process began in his life, helping him grow spiritually and learn to use his own gifts, which then impacted others. All four key components of a disciple-making culture were evident in Greg's life.

Stories like Greg's can happen at your church too. When a disciple-making culture is intimately woven into a church body, momentum really starts to pick up. Intentional leaders release peo-ple in these environments to be the very disciple-makers Jesus has called them to be. Together, we are able to spread the gospel as Jesus intended. I have watched Greg as he follows Jesus and allows God to stretch his faith. Greg is just one of more than a hundred people in our first three years as a church plant who became what I would call "disciple-makers." These leaders are actively making disciples and will release others to do the same. By the grace of God, I am watching God cultivate the fruit of disciple-making in the midst of our church culture. What a beautiful thing to watch!

Before we move on, I want to encourage you today: You can do this! Regardless of how many anniversaries your church has celebrat-ed or whatever role you have at your church—whether you are on staff, an elder, a volunteer, a deacon, or a regular church member—you can begin living out a disciple-making culture from a convic-tion of who you are as a disciple of Jesus.

In the coming chapters, I'm going to walk you through the four key components of a disciple-making culture that we outlined above: biblical foundation, intentional leadership, relational envi-ronment, and reproducible process. I use Scripture, stories, and real-life examples along the way. The stories come from churches I've had the opportunity to coach in some way, and from my own church. For most of these stories, I have changed individual and church names and simplified the details in order to maintain their anonym-ity. The few stories with names that I have not changed are about close, personal friends and co-laborers, like Tommy, Greg, Laura, Aaron, Judy, and Danny and Melissa. I use every story and Scripture in an effort to help you better understand how to create a healthy disciple-making culture. As I do, let me challenge you to start with *yourself*. With each turn of the page, allow God to move in your heart and cultivate something within *you*—and then throughout your church. Change happens one step at a time, so let's get started!

Key Component 1

BIBLICAL FOUNDATION

*How to Establish a Biblical Foundation
for Disciple-Making Culture*

1

DISCOVER IT

Discover what the Bible says about
disciple-making culture.

Over the years, I have had the opportunity to attend dozens of conferences, and I've had hundreds of conversations with pastors about disciple-making. One thing that leaders rarely talk about or seek after in their church is *the culture Jesus created*. Jesus' culture is an interesting thought, isn't it? The truth is that Jesus didn't just make disciples in a vacuum; he developed a culture of disciple-making among his disciples, and that culture transferred directly to the early church. This reveals the reproducible process at work in the early church as they received disciple-making culture from Jesus' disciples.

"Sniff the Dirt"

To truly experience something, one must get out and do it. My grandfather, a farmer, used to say, "If you want to do something, boy, you gotta go sniff the dirt." He was telling me to go get my hands dirty with whatever it is I wanted to do. Get close to it and experience it. To discover and create a disciple-making culture we must do the same.

When I talk with pastors or leaders who serve in a church, most of them lack a hands-on, practical understanding of how to make disciples, let alone a whole culture of making disciples. Many leaders—more than I can count—have said to me, "I have never been discipled and I do not know how to make a disciple." Reflect on that statement for a moment. When have you been there, even as a leader? If I asked you how to disciple someone, would you know what to say? How can the church, which is the people of God, ever succeed at the Great Commission if we, especially those of us in leadership positions, have never seen how to live it out or replicate it in someone else? We need a biblical foundation in order to experience lasting change.

The Original Coach

I had the opportunity to play football in high school and during a short stint in college, before a career-ending injury dashed my hopes of NFL stardom. Despite my disappointment about that, playing football has afforded me the opportunity to use my experiences in sports as I coach my kids in the sports they love. While coaching my boys' football team, for example, I made some observations about the importance of understanding the foundational concepts and goals of a task. They were in sixth grade at the time, and the range of maturity, talent level, and understanding among their team members was drastic. Some boys demonstrated high-competency levels, and others, well, not so much. Yet each boy knew the basic rules of football, the general objectives of the game, and how to win. They may have differed in skill level, but they all had a fundamental understanding of how the game worked.

Imagine for a moment an entire group of players wearing jerseys and standing on the field but having very little knowledge of how to play the game. They know some of the language but have no idea how to work together as a team, execute the most basic plays, or attempt to win the game. Complete chaos would ensue if we just threw those players onto the field and said, "Go play football." Unfortunately, that's how it often looks when it comes to disciple-making in the church.

We often try to make disciples of Jesus, but we don't go beyond current strategies, programs, and methods. We neglect creating *culture*. How do we expect results when we leave out this key part of the process? Jesus created a certain culture among his disciples, and we must replicate that culture if we want to see the type of success the early church experienced. Think about the change he created: His disciples had no experience in teaching anyone anything besides, maybe, how to fish. Yet Jesus spent over three years cultivating a disciple-making culture by "coaching" his disciples as they practiced fishing—for people. He showed them what this looked like before asking them to do it. We cannot expect success from our churches when we neglect culture. Without a culture of disciple-making, you might make a few disciples here and there, but only a culture of disciple-making creates lasting impact.

> *Only a culture of disciple-making creates lasting impact.*

The life of Christ clearly reveals that Jesus called his followers to make disciples, not just converts. Jesus frequently referred to Scripture as he laid the foundation for disciple-making. He spent countless hours with his closest disciples as they traveled, ate together, and engaged in deep relationships with one another. He also demonstrated intentionality with everything he did and imparted a process that led his disciples to reproduce the very culture he modeled. Intentional leaders must preach Christ's gospel and the life he modeled and use these as the seedbed of cultivating a disciple-making culture. We must lay this ground-work and nurture it from the beginning.

So if the purest form of disciple-making culture is exemplified in Jesus' earliest disciples, we can see from his disciples' writings (and those around them who wrote the New Testament) what life with Christ was like. That's why we turn to the Bible to discover how to cultivate the most effective culture for disciple-making. We could start in many places in the New Testament for this, but let's look at the life of Christ first.

The Four Key Components in the Life of Christ

We can see disciple-making culture's four key components in the life of Christ.

Biblical foundation. First, and probably most obvious, is that even before the New Testament was written, Jesus grounded his disciple-making efforts in the Bible. Today in the church, in order to cultivate healthy culture, we must emulate the biblical principles that Jesus lived out. We cannot simply implement any methods we choose. It is worth mentioning again that chasing popular programs or adopting worldly leadership models may create temporary results, but they will not build a healthy culture of sustainable disciple-making.

Intentional leadership. As I mentioned in the introduction, disciple-making requires intentional leaders who are willing to be personally committed to consistently living out the values they want to see in their church's culture. Like Jesus, these leaders must be committed to pruning and shaping the culture as it develops, teaching values and definitions to the whole church, and identifying and pursuing other leaders and influencers who can instill culture while they lead as well. Without intentional leadership the culture will be diluted and become something it was never intended to be.

Relational environment. We see that Jesus created a relational environment to foster healthy disciple-making. Like a healthy plant, disciple-making thrives in healthy soil. The relational soil that Jesus prepared was a safe, authentic, honest, and, most of all, loving community (more on that in the next chapter). This relational soil is what provides the nutrients for spiritual fruit. Imagine for a moment that Jesus *did not* create a relational environment. Let's pretend he was harsh, quick-tempered, aloof, distant, and even impatient. The gospel would lose its power, and the culture would become much more like that of the Pharisees he rebuked. Jesus built a relational environment into his disciple-making culture because it was an extension of the gospel he preached. Just like it did in Jesus' day, this healthy soil still helps relationships grow and become strong branches to support disciple-making fruit and reproduction.

Reproducible process. Disciple-making culture flourishes through a reproducible process as leaders transfer their values to the next generation through training, equipping, and releasing them to lead in new groups, new ministry areas, and ultimately in new church plants. Jesus allowed the disciples to practice ministry while he observed them, which is a major key to creating a reproducible process all along the way. He gave them opportunities, knowing full well that one day, empowered by the Holy Spirit, they would carry the movement forward. The culture he created was one that could be reproduced in others. The entire book of Acts exists because within his culture of disciple-making Jesus had a reproducible process. And we are an extension of that process. We are now living in Acts 29, you could say.

Now, let's examine the culture of one of the earliest churches influenced by the disciples. The church in Thessalonica clearly reveals the biblical foundation for the other key components.

Disciple-Making Culture in Thessalonica

In Paul's first letter to the Thessalonian church, he praises them for the incredible model they have become in the face of persecution. We know from what Paul writes that they had a particular church culture of living out the gospel and being disciples. Paul encourages them for how they have preached the gospel, specifically commending them as "imitators" (another word for "disciples"): "And you became imitators of us and of the Lord, for you received the word in much affliction, with the joy of the Holy Spirit, so that you became an example to all the believers in Macedonia and in Achaia" (1 Thess. 1:6–7, ESV). They "imitated" Paul, his disciples, and the Lord. This is disciple-making language. They created and lived out a culture that promoted the very life Jesus modeled for the Twelve. They were simply doing what Jesus had demonstrated.

Biblical foundation. We find Paul's foundation for the gospel he passed on to the Thessalonians in his other writings. He describes himself as "a Hebrew of Hebrews; as to the law, a Pharisee" (Phil. 3:5, ESV). As such, he would have studied the Old Testament writings his entire life. He also makes it very clear that his gospel came straight from Jesus: "For I would have you know, brothers, that the gospel that was preached by me is not man's gospel. For I did not receive it from any man, nor was I taught it, but I received it through a revelation of Jesus Christ" (Gal. 1:11–12, ESV). Paul did not invent his own plan of salvation or process of discipleship. As a Pharisee, Paul adhered strictly to the Jewish law found in the Old Testament; then, as a servant of Jesus Christ, Paul adhered strictly to the gospel as revealed to him directly by Jesus himself.

Intentional leadership. With all the technology and social media available today, I watch many pastors and leaders strive to find the newest ways to grow their churches as they seek innovative curricula, books, and programs in an attempt to improve disciple-making. Creativity in problem-solving should not be ignored, and innovation can be a great thing. Yet church leaders must not look first to the most cutting-edge outreach program, the most technologically advanced new platform, or the most socially relevant curriculum. This creates what I call "shiny object culture," where leaders chase after the latest and greatest of what's popular. As such, the focus of our efforts often falls on the mechanics of the latest structure or curriculum. Unless solidly rooted in a biblical foundation, these things may provide good information, but they miss the heart of disciple-making. Rather than chase these shiny objects, we should focus on creating and living out a healthy culture that creates "imitators," as Paul calls them. I would contend that if we cultivate a culture similar to the one Paul and the early church developed (because of Jesus), we will experience results like what the early church experienced.

Relational environment. Pay close attention to the words that Paul uses here: "We loved you so much that we shared with you not only God's Good News but our own lives, too" (1 Thess. 2:8, NLT). This culture of love was passed on from Christ to the apostles, then modeled for the church in Thessalonica. It consisted of sharing not only the words of the gospel *but also their very lives.* This shows how it was deeply relational, with truth being modeled, lived out, and experienced first-hand, not just taught from a pulpit or classroom. Sharing the gospel as we share our lives is both the message and the method of Christ coming together in a culture that will greatly impact the world.

Reproducible process. Paul praised the church in Thessalonica for living out what had been modeled for them (1 Thess. 1:6–7). This gives us a glimpse into the widespread movement that grew through how they lived as imitators and as people worthy of imitation. Paul and those with him had modeled for the Thessalonian church what Jesus had lived out for his disciples. Again, notice what Paul says in

1 Thessalonians 2:8: "So, being affectionately desirous of you, we were ready to share with you not only the gospel of God but also our own selves, because you had become very dear to us" (ESV). This passage shows how Paul transferred the gospel message. He received it from Christ and passed it on to the Thessalonian church. Then, they were a model for other areas where people imitated *their lives*. Jesus was their ultimate model, and he is our ultimate model too. We could call it "a healthy disciple-making culture." This is so different than what I often see today!

Bridging the Gap

Church culture today is oftentimes different than what we see in the early church. The apostles did not sit down, like we often do, and evaluate common business practices or brainstorm what advertising plan might reach the community around them. In fact, we see in the early church very little effort to "do outreach" in the sense that we talk about it today. The early church preached the gospel and simply lived it out. That was their culture, and it was an extension of what the Twelve experienced for three years with Jesus. That transfer of the gospel message, coupled with the lifestyle in which we make disciples, is the reproducible process. While we don't have a tether connected to the first-century church, we do have their testimony in writing, and that provides a clear picture—which serves as a solid biblical foundation—for creating a disciple-making culture. The Thessalonian church offers a good example of how this plays out in one biblical text because we clearly see these components, but we can also see these throughout Scripture as a whole.

We've now established the biblical foundation of the four key components in the life of Christ and in ancient Thessalonica. In the coming chapters, we are going to examine in more detail biblical disciple-making culture as if we were going to plant a massive garden with the hopes of yielding record-setting produce. Rather than merely discussing theory, though, we will highlight practical and applicable tools too. We will explore each of the components in logical order so you can make progress toward developing a healthy disciple-making culture at your church. Let's begin with the goal of disciple-making, which is creating a culture of love. This is the focus of the biblical foundation of disciple-making culture.

2
FOCUS IT

Focus on establishing a biblical foundation for love.

I stood back and watched on a Wednesday evening as my living room buzzed with conversation. Most of the buzz was around a new couple, James and Sara, who came to visit our small group. My wife, Amber, and I have led small groups for twenty years, but this was one of those evenings that will always stick with me. Before I called everyone together to begin our Bible lesson, I stood back and observed. I could not help but wonder what this new couple was thinking and feeling. What were they feeling as people greeted them, shook hands, and even hugged them? The room was filled with a relational warmth, and I realized I was witnessing a great example of what church should be: love.

Later that night, after small group was over, I was saying goodbye to each family as they left. James and Sara were the last to leave. Amber and I stood with them on our front porch for another ten minutes, talking about our families and the outdoor activities we enjoyed. As the conversation wound down, I could not help but notice James was suddenly in tears. I had seen this type of response before, so in my gut I knew what was going on. But before I could say anything, James said, "I cannot remember a time when I felt this loved." I smiled because what seemed like normal, friendly, and authentic conversation to me, was a tear-inducing expression of love and connection for him. Needless to say, they returned to our small group the next week and became regular members.

What creates that kind of an atmosphere? I mean, how in the world is it possible for a person to experience love like never before in just an hour and a half with complete strangers? Where does that come from? It comes only from the love of God among his people.

The highest aim in Scripture is to love. The Bible focuses on no other topic more than love. In fact, the Bible tells us that God *is love* (1 John 4:8, 16). Unfortunately, while Christians talk about love all the time—and pastors preach sermons describing it—I just don't see *biblical love* practiced in the church today. I might even say that, in practice, Christlike love is mostly overlooked. Yet the type of biblical love I am speaking of must be the focus and foundation of church culture.

This kind of biblical love comes only as a result of spiritual maturity. The Bible calls us to love one another, and as we grow in our relationship with Christ, our love for others will grow. I believe that the church has fallen victim to the same issues as our secular culture: we become consumed by the busyness of life, which is so often influenced by modern technology. Relationships today are often measured by approval from others on social media platforms or by a timely response to a text. The kind of relationships that foster biblical love, though, require that we fight against the secular culture's relational unhealthiness. We must pursue a biblical love that demands we prioritize our time and actually be together. Relationships that produce biblical love for one another cannot be limited to social media or cell phones. Oftentimes as a church, unfortunately, we try to program everything, but no one can program love. Love is the result of our relationship with God and a genuine interest in authentic relationship with others.

We find all over the Gospels how Jesus expressed love. Even in his greatest conflicts, he was demonstrating love. The most commonly quoted verse in the Bible, John 3:16, even describes his love.

> *Love is the result of our relationship with God and a genuine interest in authentic relationship with others.*

Christ did not intend that the love he daily demonstrated among the Twelve stop with them; it was intended for the whole world. The love Christ shows us in the Scriptures is not some abstract, far-off, unattainable "thing." In fact, we are called to love people with Jesus' kind of love. We, the church, are commissioned to live out this love as the primary aim of discipleship.

Love in the Bible

Consider these observations about three important biblical passages on love:

- Scripture rebukes those who claim to love Christ but do not love others: "If anyone says, 'I love God,' and hates his brother, he is a liar; for he who does not love his brother whom he has seen cannot love God whom he has not seen" (1 John 4:20, ESV).
- Jesus says the greatest commandment is to love God and love others: "'Love the Lord your God with all your heart and with all your soul and with all your mind.' This is the first and greatest commandment. And the second is like it: 'Love your neighbor as yourself.' All the Law and the Prophets hang on these two commandments" (Matt. 22:37–40).
- Jesus offers a revolutionary command when he describes the kind of love we are to have with one another, when he says, "A

new commandment I give to you, that you love one another:
just as I have loved you, you also are to love one another"
(John 13:34, ESV).

Do you see how important it is that love characterizes us as disciples of Christ? Whether you are a staff member, an elder, or a volunteer within the church, your greatest commandment is to love God and others.

How are you doing with love?

Without love, our ministry efforts are worthless. Regardless of the programs we have, our budget allotment for Sunday morning services, or the size of our building, without love, we fall short of what Christ calls us to do. At the core of who we are as Christians, we are to be characterized by love—Jesus' love. Love must be the defining characteristic of church culture. Without love we are creating a culture contrary to the gospel Jesus preached.

Alternatives to Love

Problems often arise in the church when spiritual maturity is equated with biblical knowledge. We sometimes adopt a false notion that more knowledge means "I am a better Christian." Yet some of the most judgmental, harsh, and unloving people I have met in the church are those who have spent much of their lives in Bible studies. I think Paul's words ring so very true: "And if I have prophetic powers, and understand all mysteries and all knowledge . . . but have not love, I am nothing" (1 Cor. 13:2, ESV).

Biblical knowledge is important, don't get me wrong. We need to study and know the Bible, and we must teach people to learn the depths of Scripture. But to what end? To gain knowledge for knowledge's sake? So that we can point out how wrong the secular culture is? No!

It's all for love.

Love must be
the defining
characteristic of
church culture.

If biblical knowledge does not translate into a deeper relational ability to love God and others in a healthy way, then we have missed the point! Then, we become just like the Pharisees of Jesus' time. Remember the simple methodology of Jesus: He loved people even when they were unlovable. He modeled a love that reached out to people and met them where they were. Too often the church communicates to the outside world that people will only be loved and accepted once they clean themselves up. If a person dresses in a certain way and has their sin issues under control, then they can cross the threshold of a church building. What an offense to the gospel! We are to love people right where they are. That does not mean we excuse sin or ignore ungodly behavior; it means we confront sin in a loving manner. Jesus loved the woman at the well and, at the same time, spoke truth to her. Jesus loved Peter while he rebuked him. Creating a culture where we love and accept people right where they are establishes the first and most important step toward building a healthy disciple-making culture.

How to Create a Culture of Love

On more Sundays than I can count, people have stepped into our church foyer and said to me, "I just feel God here." I have often thought that a peculiar statement to make, yet I believe it is true. I believe what these people are experiencing is our church's culture of love. They are experiencing God in their midst because we are expressing, by his grace, his love that creates unity among us. It's this unconditional love that makes people feel welcomed and accepted. While love comes from a biblical foundation, it lives in the relational environment of our people.

How can we create this atmosphere in our churches? How do we live out that kind of love? In the case of our church, how did we create a culture that makes people feel like they have encountered the living God in a church lobby? It's all the same: we do this through leaders who actively and intentionally seek to emulate God's love to people in practical ways. The next question, then, is this: What does this look like in practice?

I find in the life of Christ, which my church leaders and I try to emulate, five characteristics of leaders who create a culture of love:

1. Compassion. Compassion is a dominant attribute in the life of Christ. This means that he deeply cared—and cares—for those who cannot care for themselves. I have heard compassion called "empathy in action." Compassionate people love others by getting in the mess with them and walking alongside those who have deep emotional, physical, or spiritual needs. Churches regularly offer acts of kindness: assembling supplies to help hurricane victims, giving away turkeys at Thanksgiving, and providing blankets for the homeless. These are all good things, but they're not necessarily acts of compassion.

The compassion I am talking about may begin with similar kindnesses, but it goes deeper, causing a person to connect personally with those who need to be loved. It is heartfelt action that covers needs as someone delivers supplies to a flooded home and then stays to help mop up dirty water and sort through wet papers. It goes beyond the act itself, reaches into the heart, and finds its way out through the hands. It is inviting another family to join your family for a holiday celebration. It is the love we show when we sit with and listen to the stories of a homeless veteran, or go to a hospital room late at night and hold the hands of a hurting person—all

> *A loving culture is a compassionate culture.*

with the affections of Christ. A loving culture is a compassionate culture. Cultivating compassion creates security because people know they will be cared for when times get hard.

2. Inclusiveness. Jesus made a powerful statement to all religious people when he sat with Matthew the tax collector in his house: that the gospel is for all. The early church was filled with every kind of person. Leaders must exert intentional effort to affect their church to love and include those who are not like them. Most churches in America tend to draw the moral, conservative, and cleaned-up types. If we are to reach a lost and dying world, we must be willing to be like Jesus and include those who are not like us.

This is not "inclusiveness" as the world defines it, though. We accept people *as they are* and invite them into relationship, where God transforms them and never leaves them *where they are*. I often joke from the pulpit that our church is much like the Island of Misfit Toys: we are the ones that very few wanted—the broken and rejected. The funny thing is that if all of us were honest, we would see that all of us are misfits. Without the compassionate love of Christ and his act on the cross to redeem us, we all are lost, broken, and rejected. The church should be a place that invites people in, not an exclusive social club. We are to be a place that welcomes in the sinners so that they can grow spiritually as they learn truth, are loved, and walk alongside others.

3. Sacrifice. Jesus said, "Greater love has no one than this, that someone lay down his life for his friends" (John 15:13, ESV). Death-to-self means sacrifice, and this happens daily. A life of sacrifice looks like all kinds of self-denial. For example, are you willing to be interrupted? Judy, one of our staff members, sometimes reminds me that to love people, we must be willing to be interrupted. Jesus modeled living sacrificially. We often apply the phrase "living sacrificially" to money, but I am talking about something different here—a willingness to give up our time, plans, and agendas to be with people. Rather than rush to that meeting and bypass someone who is in tears, are we willing to stop and ask if they are okay?

Sacrificial love like this means we are willing to take the time to call families that are missing from our groups or church gatherings, to visit someone in the hospital, and to take a meal to a family in need. When we live sacrificially, we express a love that creates trust. It says, "When life is tough, I will be there. I have got your back." That's Christlike love. This loving lifestyle does not mean we get out of balance and give up our own families to help others. Yet we also understand that at times we must give our time, effort, and energy to serve others. At the root of love is sacrifice, and if we want to cultivate a healthy disciple-making culture that exudes biblical love, we must be willing to sacrifice.

4. Vulnerability. This is the most difficult of the five characteristics for churches today. For a church swirling with back-biting, mistrust, and pride-filled leadership, cultivating this attribute will be tough. Being vulnerable means allowing others into our lives, and this goes beyond just being "transparent." I am talking about the kind of vulnerability that says, "I will serve you," and, "I will kneel down in front of you and wash your feet." From the highest level of leadership in the church, an attitude of vulnerability must be present.

I am not saying we should all reveal every past wrong we have ever done. I am saying, though, that we should allow people to know us. We must create a culture that communicates, "I am flawed, and I'm willing to show you my flaws. It is safe for you to reveal your flaws too." When we become vulnerable, we model and foster an atmosphere in the church where people feel loved. They feel loved because they are welcomed as they are.

5. Spirit. Loving leaders are "spiritual." I mean this in the deepest sense of the word—filled with the Holy Spirit. A loving culture creates the space where the Holy Spirit can work and where people feel safe and loved. That is where healing and growth occur. When a group of Christians is loving others in a genuine way and being guided by the Holy Spirit, we will see spiritual growth.

Cultivating a Loving Culture

So what does all this mean for you in more practical terms? Whether you're a pastor, elder, or lay leader, cultivating a loving culture starts with you. You will impact the culture by the way you love people. You must be emotionally present with your people and willing to love just as Jesus loved. Give people your full attention. Put down your phone and stop looking at social media. Get eye to eye with your people. In an age of constant distraction, you must be committed to living out the highest ethic that exists in the church—love.

Now, more than ever, we live in a time of incredible loneliness, hurt, relational pain, and confusion. When we give the gift of true and biblical love, we will see people transformed. That's how the love of God works. But this requires us to take risks. We must step out and act differently than what we often see in churches. We must put ourselves out there so that God can use us to impact others. We might risk our own "security," but we gain spiritual growth in ourselves and others. Living with compassion, vulnerability, inclusiveness, sacrifice, and a vibrant relationship with the Holy Spirit can be scary, yet we are called to be like our Savior in these ways, because he exhibited all of them in his life.

A loving culture does not require us to solve everyone's problems, nor does it demand that we throw truth out the window. Some think that to be loving we must disband truth and accept any sin that secular culture says is okay. Jesus didn't do this, and neither must we. A loving culture walks with someone in their struggle with sin. We hold the hands of the hurting because we too were once like that. You and I are the misfits, and the incredible work of Jesus Christ, and his forgiveness of our sin, demands that we love like he did. So let's be willing to do whatever we can to love those who so desperately need to experience the love of Christ.

3

FRAME IT

*Create a framework of biblical values
and common language.*

In Jesus' days, disciples considered it an honor and a privilege to follow their teacher. Not everyone made the cut! That's why disciples were incredibly grateful when they were chosen by a teacher—they knew it would be a life-changing journey. When Jesus called his disciples to follow him, his disciples surely would have felt the honor and privilege. But Jesus' disciple-making style paints a very different picture from the fame and glory the disciples may have been expecting. From the very beginning, Jesus redefined what it means to be his disciple. And this is still true for his disciples today: Jesus doesn't promise us fame, fortune, and privilege. In fact, Jesus uses ominous words to call disciples to himself, words that involve loss, sacrifice—and even death.

This is why we need to properly frame the concept of being a disciple of Jesus when we build a culture of disciple-making at our church. Jesus was

*We need to properly
frame the concept of
being a disciple of Jesus.*

calling his followers to something very different than what they had known. Like so many other concepts, Jesus redefined terms in his day, and these new terms carry with them implications even for our culture today.

In the three years that his disciples followed him, Jesus framed the concept of disciple-making in a way that instituted a completely different understanding of what it meant to be discipled. He called the ordinary and average person to follow him. More than just recite from the Old Testament, he modeled biblical truth and even allowed his disciples to participate in his ministry. What Jesus offered his followers was much more than just an opportunity to come listen to a great teacher; he shared his life with his disciples and invited them into a culture that changed their lives. That's what we must do as well. Since people today aren't used to being discipled in the first place, that's a tall order!

Establishing Clear Definitions

From the beginning of our church, our little group that God called to plant Real Life Ministries Texas knew we needed to frame the process of disciple-making as Jesus did. So we spent hours together in a living room, or sometimes a back yard when the Houston heat let up, discussing Jesus' definition of a disciple. This was hard for me because we had already done this at Real Life Ministries in Idaho, but I knew buy-in for our new church was important. We had to discover it afresh as a group—because I wanted to be lockstep with our core team. I strongly recommend doing the same with your team, whether your church is young or well-established.

Our eclectic group of about twenty people had different ideas of what it meant to be a disciple and how to make a disciple, but we all agreed that we wanted to live out and define our terms as close to those in the biblical framework as possible. And not just by definitions on a page but also *by how we lived out those definitions.*

Several people from our group came to the table with a common definition of a disciple we see today, what I call "the classroom" concept. A "disciple" in this understanding is someone who memorizes Scripture and studies the Bible. There is nothing wrong with either of those things—in fact, they are important—but the life of Christ and the culture he formed went way beyond Sunday morning class or Wednesday night Bible study. So as a group, we all worked hard to define and then live out what we meant when we asked others to join us in cultivating a disciple-making culture within this new church plant. My job as the lead planter was to ensure that this happened. I needed to frame the biblical foundation for our culture by establishing a biblical context with clear, unified definitions.

Getting on the Same Page

I remember how important it was for my football coach to clearly frame the words we used and the definitions behind those terms. I vividly recall arriving on my college campus and reporting for football practice as a freshman. Guys from all over the United States were making their way to the practice facilities. As a rookie I was nervous. It was early in the morning, and the August sun was already making the air hot and sticky. Two-a-day practices were about to start, and I was sweating from anxiety and temperatures in the high 90s.

The jump from high school to college football meant everything that had once been familiar was about to change. The tension of excitement and fear wrestled around my heart, and I hoped I would not die on the first day or make a complete fool of myself. Yes, we'd be playing football, but an entirely new team culture lay ahead of me. *Would I fit in? When a coach asked me to execute a drill, would I know what to do? When the coach called plays, would I know what he was asking of me?* Questions like these swirled in my mind. Had it not been for the clarity found in the playbook, I might have quit. We were tested for two days, given all our gear, and by our first practice, everything was a blur. Coaches were screaming, everyone was running around the field, and all the freshmen were trying to adjust to the fast-paced world of college football.

I will never forget the most difficult part, and it wasn't the physical demands, joint-rattling hits, or pace of practice. Those quickly fell down the list. Communication became the name of the game and skyrocketed to the top of the list as the most difficult aspect of college football—because it was more mental than physical at that point. Adjusting to new language and definitions of terms shook my confidence, and I needed help. I needed some frame of reference to guide me through the haze of playing a new game.

That's why I was so thankful the coaches put a playbook in our hands. It took a while to get all the plays down, but from the beginning, along with my classroom studies, learning the new football vocabulary was at the top of my to-do list my freshman year of college. I felt like I was starting over with everything I knew and understood about football.

That's how it is with church culture. As you begin to frame a new disciple-making culture at your church, people will feel like you're handing them a new playbook. That's okay; in fact, it's normal. In order to cultivate thriving disciple-makers, it is critical that everyone in your church understand the key words you use and how you define them. So form the playbook with your team, not on your own in a silo. Then, communicate it well to the whole church.

> *Everyone in your church must understand the key words you use.*

Consider how important this was for a new church like ours. Our little group that met in a living room would soon grow, and many new families would join our church. Sure enough, new believers and long-time church goers alike soon came to our church with either no understanding, or a preconceived understanding, of the terms we were using. Somehow we had to align them! That's what "framing" a culture of disciple-making means: putting it all into a framework that makes sense. Framing starts with leaders. Staff members and key lay leaders need to clearly understand, define, and live out your mission-critical terms, otherwise your effectiveness will flounder. Settling for an unclear or loose frame creates a culture of confusion, where a congregation hears the words you're using but doesn't understand them or live them out. Why? Because when people don't understand what to do, they have a hard time doing anything at all.

Define Your Terms

Several months ago, I received a call from a man I will call "Dave." Over the phone I could hear Dave's excitement as he shared with me his calling to plant a church with several others. He wanted to meet with me so he could ask me questions about what God had taught me in my journey. He was familiar with Jim Putman from Real Life Ministries in Idaho and the work God had done in all of us as part of our network of churches over the years. We booked a meeting at our church with him and his four team members.

At our meeting time two weeks later, my staff team and I greeted Dave and his team at the front of our building. After we introduced our teams and chatted over coffee, I could tell that small talk was over. Dave wanted to get right down to business. His expression beamed with intensity, and his speech quickened with an eagerness to understand how we had gone from five families meeting in a house to over 600 regular attendees in our first two years. The four others with him seemed just as eager to hear the story. There we sat, my whole team with his whole team.

After briefly sharing some of the back story and my personal journey, I began to talk about our unity and clarity around the definition of the term "disciple" and other key terms. I told him about our hours of working through and wrestling with terminology. The more I shared with him about the culture we had created and what it looked like to live it out, the more impatient he seemed to get. My concern grew because, from his facial expressions, I got the sense that he was missing the point.

So I stopped and asked him, "What are you hearing me say?"

Dave replied, "You've defined a disciple. Yeah, I get that, and we as a group have already done that. I want to understand *what systems or curriculum* you are using that have helped you grow so fast." In that moment, I was proud of two things: first, how my team sat quietly and did not say anything, and second, that I did not spit out my coffee at his answer!

I took a deep breath and replied to him with an on-the-spot assignment. I knew that this assignment would make him see how his team was not aligned. I knew they were not aligned by two observations: one, by seeing the expressions on their faces as Dave described how well his team knew the vision of their church, and two, by listening to how they talked as a team. During our brief small talk right before the meeting time and during our coffee chat, I had asked questions about their progress and received an array of answers. Each member of his team was excited, but as a team, no two of them seemed to be on the same page. I had asked one person in particular about their definition of a disciple, and he'd looked completely confused. So I was prepared for a moment of potential revelation for them.

I pushed my chair back from the table and looked at their team's expectant faces. They were convinced I was about to unveil the holy grail of curriculum that would double the size of their congregation. Instead, I replied, "Before I answer your question about curriculum, I would like each of you to write on a piece of paper your definition of a disciple."

The pastor nervously looked around at his team and clicked the pen in his hand. They all began to scribble on the paper in front of them. How many different answers do you think they wrote between the five of them? If you guessed five, you are right. The pastor's face turned red, and as each answer was read aloud, the pastor's face became a deeper shade of red. This exercise revealed the point he needed to understand. Sensing both Dave's embarrassment and anger, I jumped in: "Dave, I did this exercise to make a point about people in general, not about your team. We as leaders often make huge assumptions that once we say a term, or even preach about it once or twice, then our teams, leaders, and members should have the concept locked in forever. But nothing could be further from the truth."

He understood what I was saying and accepted that they had some work to do. The beginning of the conversation we had with Dave and his team completely changed the direction of the visit, as well as their expectations for the rest of our conversation. They came in expecting to be handed a curriculum or a staffing structure that would give them a roadmap for disciple-making. Instead, I shifted the focus of our conversation away from the "mechanics" of disciple-making toward the idea of *culture*.

Words Have Meaning

The mistake Dave and many leaders make is assuming that they've already laid the foundation for cultivating a culture of disciple-making. But leaders have to be able to articulate a clear definition and personally live out that definition to properly frame a culture of disciple-making. Typing out a doctrinal statement or even writing a slogan on a bulletin is not enough to shape an entire church culture. Some say that we must hear something 1,000 times to really own it. Think of how many times and in how many ways Jesus defined for the Twelve what it looked like to be his disciple. Everything Jesus did pointed back to being his disciple. Again, culture is a way of life that stretches beyond what we could ever scribble on a page. Imagine if Jesus had asked the Twelve to be his disciples but never gave them a framework for what that would look like. Being his disciple would have lost its unique meaning.

If you were to ask a total of ten staff members or leaders in your church to define a "disciple," would they all define it the same way? Or would you get ten different answers? Cultivating a disciple-making culture with a biblical foundation requires that we define and use biblical terms, which is what God, the author of the Bible, intended for us. Consider how Jesus clearly framed being his disciple in Matthew 4:19: "And He said to them, 'Follow Me, and I will make you fishers of men'" (Matt. 4:19, NASB).

In this passage, we see the definition in the invitation: a disciple is one who is *following* Christ, being *changed* by Christ, and on the *mission* of Christ. Now, Jesus' call to follow him isn't a definition as we talk about definitions today, but in his culture, it served as his definition. He framed disciple-making early and often. In fact, Jesus spent over three years giving an absolutely crystal-clear picture of not only what it means to be his disciple but also *how to make disciples*. So when he gave the Great Commission to his disciples, they knew and had context for exactly what the call to follow Jesus meant and how to accomplish it. Jesus framed it, and even now, as his disciples who follow his method (not just his mission or message), we too must frame it.

We use the Matthew 4:19 passage (cited above) to frame disciple-making in the Real Life Ministries Texas culture, but that's not the only way to do it. There are different ways to frame it with a biblical foundation, and each church must use contextual language, but it must all go back in some way to following Jesus as he defines it. We keep our definition from Matthew 4:19 in front of our people all the time. I preach sermons on it, we train leaders using it, and we consistently discuss it in staff, elder, and volunteer meetings. "Disciple" is defined and remains a constant for us as we shape our culture of disciple-making.

My team and I described for Dave (from the story above) how we live out our definition of being a disciple and how we model for those in our church what it looks like to *follow*, be *changed* by, and be on the *mission* of Christ. We also discussed other critical terms that must be defined, framed, and lived out to have a healthy culture. Dave eventually came to the realization that their culture was hindered because he expected his team, along with their average churchgoer, to know, live, believe, and agree to their leadership's definition of terms without clear communication about these definitions.

Dave's story is common among church leaders today: they often want strategy, tactics, and curriculum, but what they really lack is a *culture of disciple-making*. In order to truly focus on culture, we need to explicitly define the terms which establish and support the framework of our culture. The two terms leaders must start with are "disciple" and "gospel." We have defined the term disciple (above), and for gospel, I recommend a powerful book called *The Discipleship Gospel* by my friends Bill Hull and Ben Sobels.[1] This is an excellent resource for helping you define the gospel.

The Gospel We Preach and the Disciples We Make

I caution you to not skip over defining the gospel too quickly. Getting your church's understanding of the gospel right is vital to the culture because it has to do with our personal understanding of *the why of discipleship*. I realized the importance of this in a very clear way during a conversation I had with a man I met in the early days of our church plant.

We met at one of my daughter's softball games since his daughter was on the team as well. He and I quickly struck up a friendship because we had many things in common, including our love for the outdoors and our faith. We exchanged phone numbers, and I invited him to coffee at my favorite coffee shop. Time went on, and we began to spend time together outside of our girls' softball games—lunch here, coffee there—and our conversations gravitated toward the church God had called me to plant and our personal theology. I thought he might be interested in joining the ministry of our church, until one day while we were riding together on our way to have lunch.

On this casual car ride, he suddenly made a statement that Christians must do works to "earn God's grace." *What?!* I thought. I heard the brakes screech in my mind. I asked him, "What do you mean by 'earn God's grace'?"

"Well, I mean that unless I do certain things in my life," he said, "I just do not believe that God could really save me."

For the next two hours, we sat in a parking lot and discussed God's grace and how grace is a free gift. Regardless of the Scriptures I used or the passion with which I spoke, he refused to even entertain my perspective. While we both had a deep theology, he held a deep, staunch, and works-based salvation position. Because of his upbringing and certain events in his life, he just could not see the grace of God as a free gift. We still remain friends to this day, but unfortunately we agreed to disagree, and thus parted ways in our ministry paths.

Before we can effectively cultivate a Jesus-style disciple-making culture, we need to ensure our gospel comes from Jesus and nowhere else. It's not just about the gospel, though; how we define all the major, foundational terms of our church will provide infrastructure for our culture. It's like my college football team when we had to understand what a coach meant by a term he used. When a play was called, I and ten other guys had to be unified on what to do. A healthy culture needs unity around the critical terms. This is not just terms like "gospel," "disciple," and "discipleship," but also terms like "relationship" and "small groups." Clarity on the definitions of these terms and how to live them out is what builds our biblical foundation for how we function. This practice significantly impacts the culture we create.

I can only imagine what life would have been like for me if I had arrived at practice as a freshman without ever having seen the playbook. The coaches would have expected me to know all the plays, terms, and calls on our team, but I would have been completely lost. The gospel is page one of Jesus' playbook, and we've got to start there so that we don't get lost.

In *The Discipleship Gospel*, which I mentioned above, Bill Hull and Ben Sobels write about the importance of defining the gospel and how that determines the disciples we make: "The gospel you preach determines the disciples you make."[2] This statement has great depth to it, and when we lack a clear definition for what we do, we can miss our target and end up creating something we never intended to create. In fact, their book also offers a definition of what they call "The Discipleship Gospel," and this definition includes following Jesus with the call of the gospel message itself. Without this, we're missing out on the whole picture. Part of the reason we have trouble making disciples in the church, they conclude, is that many people *don't even believe that's what they signed up for when they accepted the Good News of Jesus.* So we must deal first with the gospel, then go to culture. This is all part of framing the gospel.

The primary issue at hand is this: our definitions do not always match the reality of the way Jesus intentionally lived his life and discipled others. We face an enemy who wishes to destroy us, and his choice weapon is to confuse language as he sows seeds of discord at the thought level. For a healthy culture of disciple-making to exist, we must have clear language. As leaders, we must teach this, speak about it often, and live it out on a consistent basis. These practices are how we frame it, and the result, by the grace of God, is a successful disciple-making culture with people who function as a team. It's not just framing it that counts, though; it's also sticking to how we frame it, which can be even more challenging. Over the long haul, framing it only matters if you adhere to it, which is what I cover next.

Key Definitions for a Disciple-Making Culture

As you finish this chapter, I recommend you utilize a worksheet we created called "Key Definitions for a Disciple-Making Culture." This worksheet contains a sample list of critical words with definitions to help you and your team create your own definitions of critical terms. Visit **himpublications.com/culture** to download this document.

By now, you should better understand that rarely do people offer clear definitions of key terms. To intentionally keep your church's focus on disciple-making culture, you must frame the words you use in a way that people can easily understand and repeat them. Your people must know how you define terms. This can be difficult to do! That's why we created this worksheet with sample definitions for important terms. This exercise goes beyond doctrinal statements and helps you and your team get practical about clarifying definitions. Visit **himpublications.com/culture** and download this document that will help you create clear definitions for your church or ministry.

4

ADHERE TO IT

*Develop structure and leadership processes
that adhere to biblical values.*

During a visit with Amber's family in another state, it really hit home for me how important it is to stick to what your team has decided, as you frame discipleship with definitions. One Sunday, Amber and I went with her parents to visit a church they were considering attending on a more regular basis. This church had taken over an older building, and we could see signs of remodeling projects. Walking in, we smelled fresh paint and new carpet. Evidence of restoration encouraged me as I anticipated a great morning of worship with my family.

We stood in the lobby trying to figure out where to go, clearly looking like visitors. I remember being struck by incredible irony. On the wall of the lobby was painted, "Family Life Church," then on a separate line, "Where no one stands alone." The irony was that with a declaration like that on the lobby wall, visitors should expect to be immediately and warmly welcomed by greeters. But we stood in the lobby alone and couldn't see a single greeter, or even a friendly face—someone to help us know where to go. Other couples wandered by us with similar not-sure-where-to-go looks on their faces. I could hear music playing from behind a set of double doors that several others were going through, so I could only assume it was the main gathering space. I saw one couple who appeared to know the routine, and they were headed toward the double doors. I looked at Amber and her parents and said, "Follow me." At the door of the sanctuary someone handed us a small, folded bulletin. We went in, sat down, and waited for service to start.

I vividly remember this day not because of what the preacher said or because of the worship music but because I perceived their lack of commitment to one of their core essentials, which was presumably so important, that they had painted it on their wall! My point here is not to criticize this church but to identify a deeper, important and consistent issue I see in churches across the board. I'm sure no one in the church we attended that day *wanted* us to feel lost or unwelcomed. I bet they had every intention of helping us feel welcomed. But their intentions didn't produce their hoped-for results.

I know how this is! I can be that crazy-busy staff person trying to pull off the Sunday service. I too have walked past someone without thinking about whether it was their first time at our church. I hope this is rare, though, and not the norm for me. Normally, my staff and I aim to intentionally welcome people and be curious about each person we encounter in our church lobby.

My point here is that too often we write things on a bulletin or paint them on a wall, but at the end of the day they are just words—a slogan we hope to achieve or a culture we wish existed. As a reminder when we talk about culture, we're talking about *the consistently observed characteristics of a group*, not what you see when you catch people at their best, or conversely, when you catch them at their worst. Cultivating a disciple-making culture requires us not only to know what we value but it also requires us *to live out and adhere to our values over the long haul.*

Avoiding Culture Shift

Just as we get our core definitions about the gospel and disciple-making from Jesus, the values we establish for our

> *Cultivating a disciple-making culture requires us to live out and adhere to our values over the long haul.*

churches must be biblically based too, and we must stick to them tenaciously. The worldly culture fights disciple-making culture tooth and nail. If we do not undergird our values with Scripture and nurture those values, weeds will creep into the garden and stifle our growth. Even an imperceptible shift will, over time, lead a church in the wrong direction, and we will not hit our targets. We must persistently inspect the culture to know if we are being choked out by weeds. To be a disciple-making church, we must aim for making biblical disciples—then stay the course. I believe this so strongly that I wrote a book titled *Stay the Course: Seven Essential Practices for Disciple-Making Churches.* I briefly explain the "essential practices" from that book in this chapter (below), but I recommend that you and your church's leadership team read that book as a whole and discuss the questions in it for further insight.[3]

Making Values Foundational

Before we ever filed the 501(c)(3) documents for Real Life Ministries Texas to become an official church, I intentionally focused on helping our core group live out our particular set of values. While we worked through these values together, I made sure to incorporate them into our team discussions, and we began to weave them into the everyday life of our church. Even the first job descriptions we developed for our staff used these values as a structure for what we expected them to live out. We now hire and regularly evaluate staff based on their demonstration of these values. We select elders who embody these values in their lives in addition to fulfilling the biblical mandates for eldership which Paul describes in Titus and 1 and 2 Timothy.

The challenge for our church and for yours, once we have clearly defined values, is being clear about *how to walk out these values in our particular context*. That's why I emphasize processing these things with your team, so that when it comes to adhering to biblical values, you'll have buy-in from your team. All of this ensures that your foundational values become part of your culture. We must adhere to these and live them out at the highest levels of the church (staff and elders) before ever considering painting them on a wall or printing them in the church bulletin.

To steward well our early and rapid growth at Real Life Ministries Texas, we expected the core team we began with and those who joined us over the course of the first few months not to just live out our values but also to pass on these foundational values to others. In an attempt to brighten up the previously abandoned and very drab space in which our church met, we did actually end up painting our values on a wall in our first building. Our commitment to those values, however, didn't stop with stencils and paint! We structured men's, women's, students', and even kids' gatherings around our values and the scriptural basis for them. We aligned sermon series and small group curricula so that everyone in the church was immersed in the language and learned how to practically apply our values. We still do these things.

We all need to work hard to effectively communicate and transfer our values to others so that we can establish and maintain our disciple-making culture. This is true for new churches like ours, and it's even more important for established churches! If values do not become common beliefs which drive behavior, beyond just that of the staff and elders, the culture will not be healthy, and disciple-making will surely suffer.

Identifying Biblical Values

As pastors, leaders, and volunteers in the church, we are not called to be random; we are called to be intentional, purposeful disciple-makers who cultivate a culture of disciple-making. In order for us to do that, we must know exactly what we value and how to live out those values. Values are what you keep as standards or hold with the highest regard. They are the principles that govern the life of your church culture. I recommend a simple, four-step process to help you guide those around you so you can all adhere to the biblical foundations of disciple-making values:

1. *Articulate* disciple-making values clearly and consistently.
2. *Teach* and *equip* leaders to live out those values.
3. *Inspect* the outcomes to see if the values are actually being lived out (as you are honest about gaps and failures).
4. *Celebrate* when your values are displayed.

Okay, now that you have the process, what are the core disciple-making values you should adhere to? I referenced my book *Stay the Course* above, and it contains seven essential values, or "elements" as we sometimes call them. In that book, I describe these essential elements as "guardrails" which keep a church on the road of disciple-making. I list these guardrails below, along with a simple definition of each, then give examples of how you can live out each value. While it's important to read the full treatment of these essential elements in *Stay the Course*, what I've included here should get your wheels spinning about how to begin thinking through and taking action toward implementing these core disciple-making practices in your church. You might use several of mine, reword your own, or even create new ones. Most importantly, create a list of values that act as guardrails to keep your culture on course toward disciple-making.

Our Seven Essential Values

1. Abide in Christ (John 15:4–7). Every person in our church learns to have and grow in their personal relationship with Jesus Christ, which transforms the way they live in their home, church, and the world around them. Disciples walk closely with Jesus and abide in him so that they may live their lives to the fullest in Christ (John 15:5–6).

Tips for emphasizing this value:

• Encourage people to spend personal time with the Lord. To effectively live out a disciple-making culture, we all must be connected to the source. Ministry can be spiritually demanding, and through abiding in Christ, we are filled so that we have something to offer others.

• Talk about it. Naturally weave open and honest conversations about your walk with Jesus into regular discussions with your leadership teams, staff, and the church as a whole. It may take time to develop this habit and level of authenticity, so don't stress if it doesn't come quickly. Keep conversations about this alive and active by encouraging people to ask each other, "How is your walk with Christ?" Give one another the freedom to be transparent, vulnerable, and honest about your struggles. Lead this by example. Celebrate when your walk is going well and look for opportunities to encourage others in difficult times.

• Participate in life-giving relationships with others. Don't miss this significant concept: we are not only to abide in Christ but also in his body, the church. We need relationships that help us remain spiritually healthy.

2. Reach the Lost (Luke 15:1–10). Sharing Christ with someone who is lost, or "spiritually dead," initiates the disciple-making process for that lost individual. We must align our lives with the Holy Spirit as he draws those around us into a relationship with Christ.

Tips for emphasizing this value:

• Look for opportunities to invite the lost into relationships. Whether at small group, a family barbeque, or an all-church event, place value on and encourage invitation in your culture. The "build it and they will come" mentality is not what Christ modeled. Be willing to invite and "go after" the lost.

• Encourage the people in your church to be aware of those around them who might be spiritual seekers. Much like abiding in Christ, you can include this essential element in your everyday conversation. Challenge your people to go after their friends, family, and coworkers.

• Weave into the fabric of your culture prayer time for the lost. Whether it's during prayer events or in every Sunday morning service, take time to pray for those who do not know Jesus. This essential element will help you navigate what to focus on and how to encourage your people.

3. Connect the Unconnected (1 Thessalonians 2:8–12). Connecting every person in our church in a deep and meaningful way to Jesus and each other is another core value for us. As we disciple people, it is critical to connect them in a relational environment beyond Sunday morning, such as a small group, in order to grow in relationship with others and with Christ.

Tips for emphasizing this value:

• Meet with or call every person who is a part of your church to help them find a small group to join. If your church is large, ask your team for help. Make sure your leaders connect with every person. Keep a close watch on who is just attending services and not engaging in your church community in a deeper way.

• Cast vision and teach on the importance of being connected. Whether from the pulpit, in your membership class, or during your small group gathering, talk about how Jesus made disciples in relationship and the importance of being connected to the body.

• Build a small group structure and volunteer system that helps facilitate the connection process. Eliminating roadblocks for the unconnected is vital to help them get and stay involved.

4. Chase the Strays (Luke 15:11–32). Chasing those who have strayed from the flock is one of the clearest commands the Lord gives in Scripture to those who shepherd or oversee a group of people in the church. To adhere to a disciple-making culture, we must remember to pursue, value, and notice every person who has strayed from Christ.

Tips for emphasizing this value:

• Take notice. Instill in your culture a value of noticing when people are missing. Pay attention to those who might be hurting or have been absent, then discuss next steps with your staff, leaders, or elders.

• Follow up and call those who have been absent. Encourage those who lead a ministry or small group to call those who were missing from Sunday service or small group—on a weekly basis. When you call, check on them to see if they are doing okay. This becomes part of the pastoral system of caring for those who might have fallen by the wayside.

• Empower volunteers to visit or call people they know are missing. Train volunteers to help carry the pastoral load. This will help establish a culture in which leaders seek after strays that go missing.

5. Shepherd Toward Spiritual Maturity (John 10; Ezekiel 34). We need to intentionally help people not only learn the knowledge they need but also help them live out what they learn. We teach and instruct those we disciple so that they can, in turn, disciple others. Our goal for shepherding is spiritual maturity, which means that those we disciple are growing in their ability to love God and others. They are learning to live out their calling to make disciples and use the gifts God has given them within the body of Christ.

Tips for emphasizing this value:

• Create a safe environment in which disciples can thrive. Building a transparent culture allows those we disciple to ask hard questions and process the deeper truths of Scripture.

• Spend time with them. Disciples are not made overnight; we must spend time together in small groups or just live life together. This is exactly what we see Jesus doing in the Gospels.

• Ask questions with the intent to understand and challenge people. Jesus modeled incredible question-asking, and we are to do the same. We walk alongside people, asking questions that challenge them to learn and grow.

6. Release Them to Disciple (Matthew 28:19–20). We are called to equip God's people for works of service and release them to go and fulfill the Great Commission (see also Eph. 4:13). This is a great victory in the kingdom of God. We are not making disciples *of us*, but of Jesus Christ. We raise up and release people to make disciples, fulfilling Matthew 28:19–20.

Tips for emphasizing this value:

• Identify where a person is spiritually and what they need to grow in their faith. Once we identify where they are, we can properly equip them to grow. By spending time with them, talking with them, and observing them, we can identify their needs.

• Equip them. Train people and give them opportunities to learn based on what they are lacking. Equip them to be the best disciple-makers they can be, through formal and informal training.

• Release people to actually do what you have modeled for them. At some point, they have to get in the game and go execute. Just as Jesus sent out the Twelve, we too must send out the ones we disciple.

7. Function as a Team (John 17). At several places in this book, I refer to John 17, where Jesus prays for unity in the body. When we live out the first six values listed directly above, we should naturally become united in mission and relationship. In order for us to adhere to our mission and live it out, we must be unified.

Tips for emphasizing this value:

• Use the other six values to unite your group and remain committed to the overall mission. When your team becomes unclear or loses focus, bring your staff and leadership back to the core mission and recast the vision for why you do what you do.

• Do everything possible to clearly communicate within your teams and throughout your church community who you are and what you value. Focused and clear communication helps people rally around the mission and function well within the culture. The devil loves to play in the confusion, so keep banging the drum of the mission and your team will rally toward victory.

Applying These Values Today

In order for us to adhere to the biblical foundation that cultivates disciple-making culture, we must know what Jesus valued and modeled for us as essential parts of disciple-making. Based on my experiences, I believe the list above contains the seven key values from Scripture that the church of today needs to focus on the most. I've seen their importance in various ministry contexts in the churches where I have pastored and in many other churches we've trained through the Relational Discipleship Network.[4] Other values deserve our attention as disciples, no doubt, but I've found these seven to be essential *specifically for creating a disciple-making church.*

Whether you use any or all of these essential elements, you need to clearly identify your church's values. They must be biblically rooted in the life of Christ and how he modeled disciple-making for his first disciples. We aim to build a biblical culture, not a socially popular culture, and this goal requires *biblical* principles. It's only once we've built a culture based on biblical principles that we can truly adhere to the biblical command to go and make disciples. Now that we have the biblical foundation, we're ready to deal with where the rubber meets the road—with you, the intentional leader.

Key Component 2

INTENTIONAL LEADERSHIP

How to Intentionally Lead the Shift
Toward a Disciple-Making Culture

5
LIVE IT

*Personally and consistently live
out disciple-making values.*

"**W**hat is *that?*" I asked my friend Tommy. He looked back at me, eyes wide open and face with a look of deep concern. Sitting in his living room, we could hear what sounded like a freight train passing through his back yard. I remember thinking this must be what a tornado sounds like just before it hits. The sound grew to a roar, and our cell phones began to blare of warning signals for a flash flood.

It was August 26, 2017, and Hurricane Harvey, which I mentioned above, had arrived in Houston. Our church was not even a year old, and local weather forecasters were telling us to expect this hurricane to produce a 500-year-flood event in our already rain-weary city. I jumped up off Tommy's couch, no longer concerned about what we were watching on TV. I went to the front door, opened it, and saw rain pummeling the earth at an intensity I didn't know was possible. I could feel a nervous laughter welling up within me—the kind of laugh that comes not because something is funny but because it is simply unreal.

Even though we had been watching, preparing, and waiting for the storm for several days, the impact of Harvey was astounding. It sat off the coast of Southeast Texas like a bully: brooding, stewing, and building up an anger that it would unleash on everything in its path. Since I had spent most of my life living in the Pacific Northwest, hurricanes were something I had only heard about or seen through news reports. Now, they are a part of my personal experience. I will never forget the fury that storm released for three days over the Greater Houston Area.

This storm was truly a natural disaster, but it provided an opportunity for the culture of love at Real Life Ministries Texas to be tested. When life throws us these intense events, we see how people respond. Yes, the people of Houston as a whole rallied and cared for each other in the aftermath, which was beautiful to watch, but I wanted to see how those in our church would respond. I wondered: *How would they live out the principles we had spent the first eight months of our church talking about? Would faith translate into action beyond repairing flooded homes? Would they see this as an opportunity to live out the gospel and be disciples who embodied our culture?* All these thoughts swirled in my head as the rains poured down.

Wow, did our people ever step up and show up to serve, pray for, and love on our community! For some people at our church, this event was a spiritual awakening, opening doors for them to step out and intentionally disciple others for the first time.

When Harvey hit, our church plant was only eight months old, with around 120 people in regular attendance. Judy, one of our first staff members, took charge of organizing the details—the who, what, when, and where for our church to help the community. She ran our "command center," coordinating necessary supplies and mobilizing teams. Calls flooded in, and needs around us boggled our minds and broke our hearts.

Fortunately for us, most families in our church did *not* have substantial water damage. For the few who did, we arrived at their homes as soon as the rain had stopped and the water began to recede. We gathered supplies, rallied teams, and began the dirty work of mucking out devastated homes. Other teams from our church came together and went to help entire neighborhoods which had sustained heavy rainfall. These neighborhoods saw anywhere from one to eight feet of flood waters in just three days.

Incredible stories emerged as we served our community. The hurricane provided us an opportunity not just to serve people but also to disciple people. The difference between the two? Serving people helps temporarily; discipling people helps for an eternity. Let me offer you a striking example from Harvey of how intentional leadership can affect a group of people to make an eternal impact, which is the point of this chapter.

Transformation in the Aftermath of Harvey

Danny, Melissa, and their kids have been with our church from the beginning of our church plant, but at the time of the flood, they had little understanding of what being a disciple was all about (let alone anything about disciple-making culture). They just wanted something different than what they had previously experienced in church. When we began forming serving teams during Harvey, they jumped in to help, going with others from our team from house to house. It was through this experience that they began to see what it looks like to live out their faith. Seeing our team minister to hurting people, pray for them, and go beyond the call of duty by inviting them to join our small groups painted the picture for Danny and Melissa. They were learning that "church" went beyond Sunday morning services. Their discipleship transformation had begun.

The culture of
any organization
is driven by
the actions of
its leaders.

As we served families in both the immediate crisis of Harvey and during the weeks of recovery that followed, Danny and Melissa began to take ownership of their faith and live out the culture we all were working so hard to instill. They were moving from being typical Christians who attended church toward being disciples who reached out and cared for others. They invited those they served to their small group and our church services. Melissa invited others she knew to go with her as she served. Discipling others became a lifestyle for Danny and Melissa as they invested into the lives of those around them beyond just the Hurricane Harvey recovery period. The Holy Spirit was transforming them right before my eyes.

That time marks a huge spiritual shift for Danny and Melissa. Their faith became alive and active as they obeyed Jesus' command in Matthew 28:19–20. They were "going and making disciples." Danny is now one of our elders and disciples other men as well as anyone I know. Melissa also disciples others and helps lead our missions efforts in other countries. In just two years, this couple went from attending church on Sunday mornings to actively making disciples of Jesus. The Holy Spirit moved as this couple was immersed in a culture in which they saw living faith. They were given opportunities and challenged to exercise their faith. Our culture encouraged them to grow and allowed them to "get their hands dirty"—both literally and spiritually!

Culture Is More Easily Caught Than Taught

The culture of any organization is driven by the actions of its leaders. I know that I cannot disciple everyone, but a culture where disciple-making exists comes back to leadership. It's your leadership's responsibility to intentionally build this kind of culture. I invested into Danny and Melissa, but I wasn't the only one. In fact, without the others on our team, there would be no "culture." It takes a plurality of intentional leaders to make an impact, but change starts with you as a leader.

During the first eight months our church was gathering together, Danny and Melissa observed and felt the impact of living out their faith. I had personally spent intentional time with Danny, and he saw me living my faith. We shared with each other our fears, struggles, and successes while I coached him in areas of his spiritual walk. We shared life in small group with other guys, where we met together to study the Scriptures. Parallel to our studies, we did ministry together as I took him on hospital visits. Both he and Melissa were immersed in a culture that gave them practical, real-life examples. So when the time came and they were given the opportunity to apply what they had learned, they soared. They walked in confidence to make disciples and become influencers. They poured into the lives of new people, who became part of our church family, continuing the process of living out a disciple-making culture.

Cultivating a disciple-making culture cannot be programmed; it must be lived out. Did you catch that? We must be living out what we say we believe. We cultivate culture more by *how we live* than by *what we say*. As I mentioned above, the Gospels are filled with examples of the culture Jesus created as he lived life with his disciples. Let me share with you an example from John 13 that highlights Jesus as an intentional leader.

> *We cultivate culture more by how we live than by what we say.*

Living It Out

This example comes from when Jesus humbly washes his disciples' feet. He gets up from the Last Supper, grabs a towel and basin, and cleans their dirty feet. Regardless of Peter's confusion (v. 6), Jesus continues to live out this act of humility. Peter objects, but Jesus continues to model and live out a culture of gospel love, knowing that one day soon Peter will understand and know how to serve others in similar ways. Peter saw loving service lived out in a tangible way because love and service were part of who Jesus was, not just something he did on occasion as part of a programmed event.

Like Jesus and the early church, we must focus on disciple-making as "who we are," not just "what we do." Because of this mindset, our people rallied when Harvey hit. Without question we knew that we *must* go; loving those who need help was simply who we were as disciples of Jesus. This is a critical component, though, that you must catch: The "living it out" did not stop when the water receded and people's homes were cleared of water damage. We intentionally invited the families we met during the cleanup period into relationship with us. We invited them to small group, barbeques, and other social events we had as a church family. So even our invitation wasn't just for a one-time event, decision, or program. We used a real-life situation to invite them into a new kind of lifestyle. For example, remember Greg from my story in the introduction? It was in the aftermath of Harvey that I invited Greg to my house to hang out and our friendship began. I introduced him to several men from our church, and eventually, these men and I had his entire family over for a barbeque. They were invited to be part of our community *and our family*, not just a church service.

Soon, Greg and his wife, Laura, joined my small group. In this way, we began living life together, and God moved them and transformed their family. One year after Harvey passed through, Greg said something to me I will never forget:

> I am so thankful you did not invite me to church, because I never would have gone. You invited me to be part of something I understood and needed. I love going to church

> now, but I first experienced *what church should be* before I ever attended a service.

He was talking about our culture. These are powerful words from a man who did not know Christ two years before he spoke them. Don't get me wrong, though: Not everyone we helped had an amazing, happy ending like Greg did. Some hugged us and moved on, others already had church families, and, unfortunately, some could not see beyond their current devastation.

Harvey changed my life, as it changed millions of people's lives. God used that nasty hurricane to drive deep into my heart an understanding of disciple-making culture and the life-changing power of the gospel when a leader and a team are willing to *be* the church and intentionally live out the message we preach on Sunday morning.

Principles of Living It Out

Walking away from all of this, I learned three critical principles about intentionally living out a disciple-making culture:

1. Intentional leaders must "go." In Matthew 28:19–20, Jesus commands us to go into the world and make disciples. Intentional leaders must be willing to go, to be proactive and lead the way. Leaders must first serve others, love their community, and share the gospel through action before they expect the church as a whole to do those things. We cannot ask someone to do something we are not willing to do. We cannot delegate "going" to others. While we release others to go, we never graduate from it ourselves. When you are the first to go, you cultivate a culture and model for your people what it looks like. Once you stop going, you stifle disciple-making culture. For example, when I visit someone in the hospital, I rarely go alone. I make it a habit to take someone with me. This allows me to model for that person what it looks like to go and minister to others, and it provides time for us to talk and process life along the way. We debrief after the visit and talk about all we saw God doing. This becomes an intentional way to invest into the life of another. Once that person knows what it looks like to love, they can do it too.

I saw some fruit from my labor in this regard several weeks before writing this chapter: A man in our church went into the hospital for open heart surgery, and the response from our church caught me by surprise. My day had been hectic until that point, so I did not have time to grab anyone to go with me. I hadn't expected anyone else to be there, but when I walked into his hospital room to pray with him before surgery, four other men who attend our church greeted me. They had arrived before me and were sitting around his bed getting ready to pray. As I looked around the room, I remembered how each of these guys had gone on a hospital call with me. Now, without prompting, these guys showed up because it is simply who we are as a church. They took the command to "go" from Matthew 28, and they went. Emotions welled up in me as I saw these men caring for their friend and being the ministers Jesus called them to be. He's called all of us to be like that. They knew to be there because they had seen it, and now they were living it out too.

2. Intentional leaders must "be." Churches in our Western culture today are filled with so many different programs. Regardless of their effectiveness, what tends to happen is that churches become *programmatic.* We focus more on "pulling off" programs than on being who God has asked us to be all the time. Programs have their place, but only after culture. Oftentimes, leaders are exhausted and burned out from trying to execute programs. When a loving culture is a mere add-on, programs are exhausting and promote a culture of busyness.

God is much more interested in who we are becoming than in how many

> *God is much more interested in who we are becoming than how many programs we can fund, organize, and execute.*

programs we can fund, organize, and execute. Take, for example, the hospital visitation: Rather than create a hospital ministry or hire a part-time staff person to make hospital rounds (both of which have their place), let's first focus on building a culture in which everyone believes that they are to live out the gospel. Then, if we still need a program, let's form that program around making the culture flourish. If we focus on culture, people will run to opportunities all day because that is what has been modeled for them. They understand what the gospel says, and they embrace the lifestyle that Jesus modeled. So when a person from their small group is in the hospital, no one sits around and says, "We better call the pastor." They say, "I'm going. Who's going with me?" That's what disciple-making culture looks like when it is *who we are* not just *what we do.*

3. Intentional leaders must help people "see." Inviting people into your life helps create a culture where people can see a living example. The words you've placed on the walls and in the bulletins become real and practical—where people can see it in real life. This "live it" mentality is where the rubber meets the road. As a result, when leaders live out the culture, those who have not been in a church where Jesus' methodology exists can see it too.

Whether we're talking about Danny and Melissa, Greg, or the guys at the hospital, they all serve as examples of the power of seeing disciple-making culture lived out. The disciples saw Jesus in the flesh, not just as an evidence of God incarnate but also as a living and breathing model of the gospel. Those in our church are no different than the fishermen with Jesus: they need to see what disciple-making looks like. When you as an intentional leader live it out as best you can, you create a culture that reflects what Jesus modeled. That's living it, which helps other people see it.

Unfortunately, in the church today we have replaced "seeing" with "educating," thus creating cultures built on head knowledge alone rather than on cultures where disciples live a certain way. Our world is in desperate need of disciples who live out and create a culture of disciple-making. Whether serving people in crisis, visiting people in the hospital, or leading people in a small group, you as an intentional leader must show for all to see a practical example of what it looks like to follow Jesus in all of life. *They must see it in your life.* It's not just about action, though; intentional leaders must also use words to communicate this lifestyle, which is what the next chapter is about.

6

COMMUNICATE IT

*Capture opportunities to teach your values
and definitions to the whole church.*

I stared at my notes for Sunday's sermon feeling a bit worn out and asked my team what felt like a rhetorical question: "Do I really have to say this again?" A few of us make a habit of going through my sermon notes as a team during the week leading up to Sunday. This particular week, I hung my head in frustration. Although I had multiple points in my notes about casting a vision for disciple-making, along with our values, I felt repetitive communicating it *again*.

We had been gathering as a small church for less than six months, and I felt as though every time I stood in front of our people, I was saying the same thing. Week in and week out, I would teach about Jesus' methods of disciple-making and describe the culture he created, and I felt like a broken record. To my surprise, though, our group of people had grown in their excitement and deepened their understanding each and every Sunday, so while I felt like a broken record, it was necessary and good for our church. Each week, we had new people join us. Those on my team reminded me I had to keep banging the drum, repeating the terms and concepts of what it means to be a disciple and make disciples. Although I varied the Scriptures and biblical stories, I remained consistent in illuminating for them how the New Testament writers described the life of a disciple-maker. I knew the team was right; I just had to fight through my own struggles.

I've mentioned my dear friend Jim Putman a few times now because I learned disciple-making culture first from him. He used to repeat to me *all the time* the following words about disciple-making culture: "Brandon, we have to eat, sleep, and drink this stuff." During the season of ministry when I was with Jim, I thought he was being a little extreme, but I've come to realize by experience that he was right: we must constantly talk about this mission of how to make disciples, especially with those closest to us.

The Mother of All Learning

We know that people learn by repetition. My kids have heard me say some statements a thousand times. Oftentimes, they will even finish statements for me. The Latin phrase *repetitio mater studiorum est* means "repetition is the mother of all learning." I bring up this Latin phrase to show you how foundational repetition is—that it is found even carved onto the stone of ancient ruins!

Repetition is important for cultivating church culture because we live in a time in which many voices give opinions on what church life should look like. Once common terms at a particular church are tweaked or redefined contrary to biblical teaching, members lose sight of their true meaning. Similarly, churchgoers floating from one church to another, in and out of denominations, will find many interpretations of the same terms. This creates a hodgepodge of church backgrounds, and church leaders find themselves at a loss in trying to create any kind of consistency. We must first acknowledge that it is unrealistic to believe that we can say something once

Repetition is
the mother of
all learning.

or twice to a group of people and expect them to hear it, live it out, and apply it. Repetition is the key to learning, so leaders must understand that intentional and consistent communication to those we lead is essential for building a thriving disciple-making culture. Regardless of your position in the church—whether you're a staff member, elder, or volunteer—the words you use, and how you define, repeat, and live out those terms, impacts culture.

Calling the Twelve to follow him, Jesus came face to face with their assortment of belief systems which were inconsistent with the principles in his kingdom. Jesus confronted their beliefs on issues like how to treat the Gentiles, works-based salvation, and caring for the less fortunate. He used various means to communicate how their beliefs must change to align with God's plan. Whether telling a parable, demonstrating love by his actions, or speaking the truth outright, Jesus clearly and consistently illustrated the principles of disciple-making culture for those who followed him.

Like Jesus, we will always need to communicate what a disciple-making culture looks like; that need will never go away. Some people will get it early on—these are "early adopters." Others will have to plow through years of broken and dysfunctional belief systems from their past to truly receive it for the first time. Once one person will seem to understand, another will seem to forget. To communicate this culture, the leaders of a church must eat, sleep, and drink disciple-making culture.

Twice a year, our staff gathers all of our small group leaders together for an intentional weekend of training. Rather than writing a new introductory message every six months for these gatherings, I always begin by repeating the same message. In this message, I intentionally describe the disciple-making culture we want to live out, maintain, and invite others to join. Each time we hold these training weekends, leaders who have been with us from the beginning will come up to me and say, "Thanks, Pastor, for telling us that again. I always seem to forget or take it for granted." Plus, new leaders get to hear it too, early and often. To build and maintain culture, it's critical that intentional leaders identify valuable times to communicate and teach the biblical foundation, values, and principles that uphold their culture, and they need to do it over and over again.

Five Key Communication Venues

I've mentioned one venue for communicating disciple-making culture and leadership (biannual training events), but where else do we communicate disciple-making culture? When do we do this? Here are five key venues for communicating disciple-making culture:

1. The sermon. The most obvious place to communicate what a disciple-making culture looks like is in the main church-wide message each week. If you're a pastor or preaching minister, preach about it on Sunday mornings so your whole church gets the opportunity to hear what you believe and value. Weave throughout your message clear descriptions of the culture you have discovered and how you have framed it. In fourteen years of living in the culture of Real Life Ministries in Idaho, I learned the importance of communicating this message over and over from the stage on Sundays. Each Sunday, Jim Putman would essentially preach the same message but with a different angle. That is, every week he would give the same gift with different wrapping paper.

Sermons offer a great place to explain and unpack the fine details of disciple-making culture. As a lead pastor, I take the opportunity afforded by sermons to define terms, tell stories, and give testimonies of how various people in our church live out culture. I talk about the biblical example Jesus modeled, and I parallel it with real-life examples.

Jesus himself did something similar since he was an itinerate preacher, going from town to town preaching similar things with a unique twist. Think of the beatitudes Jesus gave during the Sermon on the Mount discourse (Matt. 5:3–12). Jesus was describing the truth of the kingdom and what it looks like to live the life of a Christian. Then, during the Sermon on the Plain, he said the same thing but framed the life of a disciple in terms of "blessings and woes" (Luke 6:20–26). Jesus communicated principles through his preaching, then continued to communicate them as he lived them out and discussed them with his followers.

2. *Membership classes.* While Jesus did not host membership classes, and some churches do not have membership classes, experience has led me to believe that for the American culture, it's important to host them. Regardless of your opinion or philosophy about membership classes, it's wise to provide a venue for introducing your theology, values, church structure—and culture. I would say it's even necessary. Both Christians and non-Christians who attend need to know up-front who you are and what you're about. This leads to better retention among visitors, and even eventually among members.

When planting Real Life Ministries Texas, we found that our membership class "101 Partnership" (we refer to our church members as "partners") became one of the most important places to communicate culture. It's just as important for established churches; new churches simply have a keen insight into this because they are so new. To communicate the culture, for example, we describe the importance of small groups and explain how disciples can be made in small groups. We talk about how we work together as a team and live out relational disciple-making in our church. We describe in detail the expectations of our culture. Without some sort of class or "front door" process, you leave people to assume or guess what you're about. In the class, we address the most critical doctrinal issues and give attendees opportunities to ask questions. We give a clear description of who we are and where we are going. We also define the key terms that provide the framework for our culture.

When the class ends, each person has a good idea of what our church is all about.

3. *Staff and elder meetings*. Most people who serve in a leadership or volunteer position in their church experience an abundance of meetings. From talking with pastors and leaders of various churches and ministries, I have found that most meetings are buried in programmatic, business-type agendas. Yes, the business of the church needs to be addressed, but I caution against church meeting agendas that prioritize business-related items over disciple-making-related items. As the head goes, so goes the body. In the church, leaders set the direction and drive the composition of the culture. If you as a church leader do not intentionally communicate on a consistent basis about a healthy disciple-making culture, your meetings will quickly erode into something they were never meant to be: purely business. We must intentionally drive the list of meeting items to reflect the importance of disciple-making culture.

As such, in our elder meetings, we discuss disciple-making culture issues. We ask hard questions to evaluate how well we are living out what we believe. For example, I use the list of "Seven Essential Values" from Chapter 4 above as a guideline for discussion. As a group, we evaluate how well we are living out those values personally and throughout the church. Some sample questions might be: "How is your personal walk with Jesus?" or, "Whom have you helped find a small group this week?" or, "What groups are preparing to branch out and create new small groups?" Continuing to push conversation and evaluation of culture in leadership meetings helps ensure that we keep the most important topics on the table, eliminating drift and holding firmly to what we believe.

4. *Volunteer gatherings*. Intentional leaders must pass on the values and principles of their church to volunteers within the church. From the very beginning of our church plant, we have intentionally planned times to gather all our volunteers. We know that people are busy and that honoring their schedules is important, especially if we want them to actually show up, so we plan each gathering months in advance. Plus, we make sure to fully utilize the time we ask of volunteers. During these meetings, we communicate and reinforce the vision, values, and principles of our church. We celebrate successes and share where God appears to be leading our church. I strongly suggest that you also plan for these times. Look ahead at your calendar and ask around to find what times work best for your volunteers. To ensure volunteers have a good experience at these gatherings, make the gathering fun and informative. Make sure to always communicate who you are as a church. Remember, you are establishing and maintaining culture, so repetition is key.

The Gospels only capture a small percentage of what Jesus communicated to his disciples on a daily basis. But these snapshots tell us what he communicated and how he communicated it. Jesus knew that broken understandings about God and his plan to reconcile mankind plagued those who followed him. As a result, Jesus tirelessly communicated something very different, and his communication helped create the culture that would forever change his disciples. Leaders in the church today must intentionally communicate in a way that paints a clear picture of what a disciple-making culture looks like. The moment we assume that everyone we lead has fully grasped and accurately lives out our disciple-making culture is the moment we begin to slide down a slippery slope.

5. Personal relationships. Plan intentional time in your schedule to be with those who play an essential role in communicating your vision and culture as a church. If you're a lead pastor, this means your staff and key lay leaders; if you're a ministry leader, this means your key team members; if you're a lay leader, this means those you're discipling. Our temptation is to make the mistake of assuming everyone in the church is communicating the vision and values like we are, using the same language and meanings, but we must never stop talking about culture. Whether it's at a coffee shop or on the golf course, we must spend time in proximity with those who are helping build culture.

Jesus stayed in close proximity to his disciples and could hear what they were saying so he could tell when they were off course in their thinking. We must do this too. If you are building a new ministry or trying to change something deeply rooted in an established ministry, do not bypass or forgo personal time with those who are doing ministry with you.

The five venues I've just outlined—the sermon, membership classes, staff and eldership meetings, volunteer gatherings, and personal relationships—are the most common and important outlets we've found for communicating disciple-making culture. Perhaps you have an alternative list of venues. Whatever the case, once you identify the primary venues through which to intentionally communicate your cultural values, make sure to maximize them to communicate most effectively. Let me show you how to do this with the following three tips. These will help you implement the important aspect of solid communication as you cultivate disciple-makers in your church.

Communicating Your Disciple-Making Values

I really want you to get this: Communicating your values clearly and effectively will result in great dividends, but offering an overly complex or confusing message can create disappointing losses too. So save yourself some headaches and learn from us about how to communicate culture:

1. Be clear and concise. Several years ago, I was asked to visit a church and give their leadership team feedback on what I saw of their culture. The pastor asked me to sit and observe a meeting with him and his staff. He began describing several different strategic approaches to disciple-making and how their team was going to try to blend them together. I'm not against learning from or borrowing from what others have built, but I immediately saw a lack of clarity descend over his staff like a veil over their faces. Confusion settled on the room, and I could tell the pastor sensed it too. But in a valiant attempt to disperse the fog, he rambled on for more than thirty minutes—to no avail.

His personal lack of clarity on key components permeated the discussion, but what's more, he married different approaches as well, which created an extensive and complicated strategic approach. His staff members were either lost in a fog of confusion, perplexed by the complex jargon, or thinking about what they would rather be doing than sitting in that meeting. Articulating clearly helps establish your culture. With clear articulation, the people in your church know exactly what you are about, then become carriers of the vision.

I also suggest that you keep it concise. Remember, people are busy, and we compete for their attention in a demanding world. When you can trim down a list of values from twelve to seven, or when two sentences will accomplish the same as twenty, do it. Clear and concise communication empowers people in your culture to pass on what you believe.

Each week, spend time discussing the sermon, upcoming events, and other gatherings with your team to ensure that what you communicate is consistent with what you believe as a church. At times, it can seem like extra work, but in the long run there will be greater freedom and ownership as a result.

2. Ask questions to check for understanding. Walk among those in your church and ask what they are hearing. This provides powerful feedback that can help clarify your communications. Each month, we invite new visitors to a dessert gathering on a Sunday evening. At one of these "Visitor's Desserts," I attempted a new way of describing our culture and what God was doing in our church. Afterward, I asked one of the visitors what she heard me say. Wow! Her response surprised me. I quickly learned that what I had thought I was communicating was way off the mark. This helped me adjust and clarify some important terminology for future communications.

3. Use testimonials. Some of the greatest communicators of your culture will not be staff members or elders but lay leaders whose lives have been changed by it. Their testimonies are the best proof that your church lives out what you say you believe. Look for opportunities to put the greatest stories of God's work in your church in front of the church body. With all of the current technology, capturing stories through video and other means can be powerful. Use all the mediums you can, even social media. Stories of how the culture impacts people help drive deep the roots of your church and help people relate to your mission.

Repeat, Repeat, Repeat

Just because you've communicated a concept in the past, don't assume everyone who has heard it recalls it. New people come into the church all the time; regular attendees miss a week here and there due to illness, vacation, or whatever; and believe it or not, those who are there may not be listening to you! Jesus repeatedly said the same things, and the early church lived out and communicated the teachings of Jesus. Repetition in your communication increases your chances to reproduce your culture. Yes, you have to keep saying the same things over and over, just like I'm doing here. Communicate clearly and often—and don't stop.

I remember a professor in my ministry master's program teaching us something about Paul that has stuck with me: Paul is often described as someone who taught a massive array of topics. He admitted that Paul covered a great deal of theological ground, but if you step back, Paul was really communicating one thing: living the life of a disciple in light of the gospel. He just said it in many different ways and addressed a number of problems that hinder us from going into the world and making disciples of Christ.

Our challenge as Christians is to stay focused and to promote a disciple-making culture wherever we go. To do this we must communicate a consistent and intentional message by word and deed. Anything that draws attention away from the central message of the gospel will require additional time and resources to correct. Effective pruning will help you avoid costly distractions. That's the topic in the next chapter, where we discover more about the role of intentional leadership.

7

PRUNE IT

*Prune away distractions to optimize
resources for disciple-making.*

Several years ago, a pastor from another church in Houston asked me to meet with his leadership team to discuss their church's transition toward becoming a disciple-making church. *(Notice a theme of curious people here? Disciple-making culture is attractive! The word gets out.)* Over the phone he explained to me how their church was floundering. He felt lost. Their team gathered a large crowd on Sunday mornings but lacked something he simply could not put his finger on. He felt frustrated and defeated, despite a good outward appearance of high church attendance. So we set up a time to meet.

After several hours of discussion with him and his staff, I had a feel for the culture of their church, and I began to ask questions. I started by asking them about areas of their church they felt were "struggling," and I used that word. You should have seen the look on the pastor's face.

"What do you mean by 'struggling'?" the pastor asked me.

"I mean a ministry that might be using resources, even a ministry that has existed for years, but in no way impacts the mission of the church," I replied.

Everyone sat in uncomfortable silence. Eyes darted around the room as some of the staff tried to read each other's faces, as though some secret poker game was going on and each one wondered who would tip their hand first. We sat in silence as the seconds ticked by, no one willing to break the palpable tension.

The senior pastor cracked. He smashed the silence with a huge belly laugh. One by one, each person on the leadership team began to smirk, and the poker faces went from grins and giggles to an all-out roar of laughter. Apparently, I had uncovered something in their culture, and I was determined to get to the bottom of what was going on. That's exactly what I told them: "So I must have stumbled onto something, or you guys have the best inside joke of all time, and I am in the dark."

"Both!" The pastor declared. He wiped the tears from his eyes, took a sip of coffee, and went on to tell me the backstory.

For more than thirty years, their church had supported their own quilting ministry. Women would gather in a large room in their church building and make quilts for the local hospital to give to mothers, babies, and ill children. The ministry shrank over the years from over forty women to seven or eight elderly ladies who were now meeting each week. The ministry was literally dying off because most of those involved had passed away over the years.

This ministry was not bad or wrong to exist. In fact, the lovingly crafted quilts were a great way to bless families. The issue was that the women leading the ministry adamantly demanded access to a certain room in the church and the right to reimbursement for the materials they used, with no discernable disciple-making impetus. Multiple times over the years, the church leadership had attempted to talk with the ladies about moving to a more appropriate location.

The requests were met with threats by the ladies of leaving the church, demands for more advertising in the church bulletin, and no compromising. The quilting ministry, run by a few volunteers, had become a legacy ministry that no one wanted to address. That's what this pastor and his team were all laughing about.

Staff members and volunteers continued to work around the quilting ministry. Leaders actually feared having a conversation with these ladies about moving the location or making other changes to their ministry. What was once a vital part of the church outreach had now dwindled to simply a nice gesture the church was making to the community. Even worse, it had become something that did not positively contribute to the disciple-making culture the church so desperately needed.

Can you relate to the situation these church leaders faced? What ministry does your church have that doesn't contribute to a culture of disciple-making? What ministries that don't support or align with disciple-making values continue to consume your resources?

The laughter from the leadership team that day was profound. It was not just about their dedicated quilters; they laughed because of their sudden realization of the true issue at hand. They knew several of their ministries were not focused on disciple-making, and in order to forge ahead, they would need to not only redirect some of the ministries but also to entirely cut some of them. They needed to prune their church in order to be more fruitful.

The Need for Pruning

Creating a disciple-making culture requires careful pruning—the ongoing process of cutting back a plant to make it healthy. It's not about the cutting away of life-sucking branches; it's about the results of the pruning. Pruning creates new growth. A plant

Creating a disciple-making culture requires careful pruning.

that has been thoughtfully pruned will often return a fuller plant that bears healthier, heartier fruit.

Amber and I bought a home three years before I wrote this book, and it had many rose bushes in the back yard. At first, these plants looked like a massive overgrown weed patch. Different weeds intertwined with the rose bushes, and branches ran wild, creating a tangled mess. Together, with gloves and pruning shears, we sorted through, cut, and discarded every weed and wild plant that was not part of the healthy rose bushes. But we didn't stop there. Once we made it through the weeds and brush, we pruned the rose bushes themselves back to the point that I was afraid we had killed the plants. Satisfied with our efforts, we stopped and waited to see if they were going to survive our barrage of snipping. Sure enough, a few months later, green buds appeared, and before long, branches were shooting out with gorgeous rose buds everywhere. The plants looked healthier than ever, and the number of roses had quadrupled.

Throughout the Scriptures we see how God trims, cuts back, and cleans up his people to produce spiritual fruit in them. Jesus gives us this picture of pruning in John 15:1–5:

> I am the true vine, and my Father is the gardener. He cuts off every branch in me that bears no fruit, while every branch that does bear fruit he prunes so that it will be even more fruitful. You are already clean because of the word I have spoken to you. Remain in me, and I will remain in you. No branch can bear fruit by itself; it must remain in the vine. Neither can you bear fruit unless you remain in me. I am the vine; you are the branches. If a man remains in me and I in him, he will bear much fruit; apart from me you can do nothing.

God prunes people on both a personal and a corporate level. In order for us to become more spiritually mature, as individuals and as a body, we must be pruned. When this happens, God is preparing us for what he wants to produce in and through us. Whether we like it or not, the Holy Spirit will convict us as the Father prunes us so we will produce fruit. Without the need for our permission, God searches the heart of his people and, with pruning shears in hand, he cuts away what is not spiritually healthy.

Consistently in conversations I have all over the globe with church leaders, I hear them say of their churches, "We have lost the art of disciple-making." They tell me how their programs that were once effective or popular no longer hold luster. Their churches have become like the rose bed in my back yard—overgrown with all kinds of plants, weeds, and even disease that fills up space but lacks beautiful fruit. What can we do about this?

Be Willing to Cut—with Love

Cultivating a biblical disciple-making culture starts with a willingness to roll up our sleeves and pick up the shears. This is part of our obedience in following the Holy Spirit as he makes adjustments to his church. Think again about the church with the quilting ministry. They identified several areas in their church that required pruning. They used great care, respect, and relational processes to gently trim, shape, and in some cases even eliminate a ministry. Rather than just walk in, make cuts, and hope everyone adjusts accordingly, they met, in love, with each person who was part of the ministry. They provided vision and explanation and slowly made adjustments.

Even so, not everyone liked it. Yes, they even had some people who, no matter how lovingly they were handled, left the church. As a leader you have to make a decision to answer honestly for yourself the following questions: *Is biblical disciple-making my primary focus or not? Is fulfilling the Great Commission more important than catering to certain people in my church? Am I willing to prune even when it might hurt? Who am I trying to please, God or man?*

It's one thing to watch God prune an individual; pruning a church, however, is even more difficult! That's why following the Holy Spirit is vital when he is calling us to make adjustments in his church. This may come in the form of letting go of a program, event, group, leader, or even a long-held tradition—whatever needs to be taken away in order for your church to thrive and multiply disciples.

To create this kind of culture, be willing to go in and cut what's not producing fruit. I know this is hard, but it's part of the leadership role that we must embrace and understand if we really want to experience change. We must understand that there is great danger when we are not willing to cut. A plant with dead or diseased branches will become unhealthy without pruning. Branches that no longer produce fruit will continue to consume vital and limited nutrients. When we

> *We must understand that there is great danger when we are not willing to cut.*

do not evaluate our churches with an honest assessment of how well each part contributes to making disciples, our churches suffer. Ministries become programmatic and demand huge amounts of time, effort, and energy, yet we see no impact on disciple-making year after year.

Pruning might mean that you have to reduce the size of a ministry or cut some of its budget. It might mean that you cut a ministry altogether. You also might need to do some retraining of those who lead or change leadership. That's a form of pruning too. What remains critical is that you are willing to do the hard work of pruning. Together with those on your team, take the steps to help your ministry be as healthy as possible.

It Starts with You

The most important thing I can say about pruning is this: *you must start with you.* Before you can look at your church and evaluate its effectiveness, you must stand in front of a mirror and look at your own life. Ask yourself, *Am I producing the fruit of a disciple-maker?* As you ask yourself this question, take heart! Remember some take-aways about the pruning process:

1. *Trust that fruit will come.* When Amber and I cut our rose bushes back to basically stumps, we both believed, at the time of pruning, that we may have cut too far, but time told a different story. Sometimes the Lord will prune us back so much that we might think it's too much, even questioning his love for us. But God wants fruit production in you and me and in his church so much that he's willing to lead us through the valley to get there. So trust that God the Father and the work of the Holy Spirit will produce fruit. This gives us the courage to do the necessary pruning to really see fruit.

> *God wants fruit production in you and me and in his church so much that he's willing to lead us through the valley to get there.*

Years ago, when I was at Real Life Ministries in Idaho, we had grown so much and had so many people involved in various ministries, we realized that some of what we were doing was not helping us make disciples. We too had ministries that had become ineffective or irrelevant for where we were, and we needed to prune. Events changed, opportunities went away, or the need was filled, and these ministries were no longer needed. We had to make alterations to several ministries, and we had to cut others. It was hard at first, but over a period of two years after that, we saw incredible spiritual growth in our people.

So what's the takeaway here? Resist the urge to implement a new program or chase the latest "shiny object" in the church world. Prune back the ministries you need to prune and wait to see what the Lord produces. Waiting can be hard. Fruit production requires having patience and giving the Holy Spirit time to work.

The church I mentioned that had the quilting ministry pruned what they needed to, then had the discipline to wait on the Lord. Even in our own lives, when God prunes back an area so that we are able to be more productive, we need to be patient. Wait and watch to see what fruit begins to blossom.

2. Remember that it's a process. My daughters play fastpitch softball. In softball, as in any other sport, you must put in hard work to excel. This requires discipline and a willingness to grind through the process. My daughter has this quote on her wall: "Hard work beats talent when talent fails to work hard." Now think of that statement with regard to disciple-making. To fulfill the model of Christ's life, we must commit to *his* process—a method and process that he commanded us to go live out in the world around us.

My daughter Olivia primarily plays the position of catcher. At one point, she decided to improve her accuracy and speed at throwing the ball to second base when someone is stealing, so she had several drills she routinely practiced. She found that some of the drills she had been using for years were not as effective as others. So she had to prune the less efficient parts of her routine and be willing to practice a new method that felt awkward and different.

One of the new drills required holding one corner of a small hand towel called a "rally towel." She would put herself in a stance as if preparing to throw, with the end of the towel replacing the position of the ball. Olivia would execute the throwing motion holding the towel instead of a ball, and at the very end, she would snap her wrist as hard as possible to make the towel "pop," like cracking a whip. I remember the confused look on her face the first few times she did the motion. But she stuck with the process, and over time, her throwing velocity improved. The process helped her remove unwanted motion and correct some of the form issues she was having. Improvements came over time, after she repeated the process hundreds of times. She cut away what did not work and saw the fruit of improved motion.

Making disciples is not about speed. The process is often long and arduous. Yet with repetition comes greater effectiveness and knowledge of how the Holy Spirit works in us to accomplish disciple-making. When we practice what we preach, we build a culture of people who know how to live out the process. That way, when we see something that is not working, it stands out, and we can take the steps to prune.

From the very beginning, we have fought hard in our church to stay faithful to Jesus' methods of disciple-making. With so many new people joining us from various backgrounds, we have had to make strong commitments to not be distracted or allow our culture to shift. Faithful diligence to the processes I outline in this book ensures that we make disciples the way Jesus made disciples and produce the fruit he wants us to produce.

3. Stick to it. Much like my daughter learned to improve her throw through commitment, I want people on my staff to be willing to remain committed to the process. I want to see the diligence that will produce fruit over time and an attitude of humility that allows for change and growth. Resist the desire to move away from the process of making disciples, even though it may become tedious, repetitive, or difficult. Remember that part of building and maintaining culture is simply a grind. Olivia wanted to do a different drill and quit the one she was doing because she was bored with it. But she stuck with it. It's the same with culture: sometimes you just have to stick with it.

Because Amber and I faithfully pruned our roses, they grew into healthy, vigorous plants with bountiful and fragrant blooms. Without regular pruning, they would become overgrown and unhealthy. Plus, they would not produce the beautiful flowers they were created to produce. Essentially, we would have cultivated a garden full of plain thorn bushes, nearly impossible to work with and not very pretty to look at either! The definition of insanity is using the same methods over and over without having the humility to change what is not working, yet expecting different results. Pruning, although hard and painful at times, is one of the most important things that the Holy Spirit will guide you through in cultivating your culture.

Pruning can be difficult work, but even with all the pruning, you still need the right environment for a plant to really thrive. Disciple-making culture is the same: you need the right environment. This is what we call the "relational environment," which is necessary to cultivate a fruitful disciple-making culture at your church. Next, I'll describe what this environment is and what it looks like in practical terms that you can start applying now.

The Prune It Worksheet

I recommend you visit **himpublications.com/culture** to download "The Prune It Worksheet" to help you evaluate the effectiveness of any given ministry in your church. This resource includes a chart with questions to help evaluate a ministry's effectiveness and how that ministry impacts culture. This will help you effectively prune what needs pruned. The goal of pruning is to ensure you and your church thrive as disciple-makers.

Key Component 3

RELATIONAL ENVIRONMENT

*How to Construct Relational Environments
That Foster Disciple-Making Culture*

8

CREATE IT

Create safe environments in which
disciple-making naturally occurs.

When I was a young pastor at Real Life Ministries in Idaho, I watched with curiosity a "spy" who was walking around our church lobby one Sunday morning. If I didn't know any better, I would have thought he was gathering data for an intelligence agency, because he held a voice recorder in his hand. As he made his way through the buzzing crowd, several of our people introduced themselves to him. He would randomly stop, hold his small handheld recorder to his mouth, and record a voice memo into it. I could have been concerned about this oddity, but instead I found myself fascinated, and somewhat weirded out, by his behavior. As I made my way over to him, he couldn't tell I was listening to his voice memos. I heard him speak into the recorder something I will never forget: "Every third person is a greeter." I couldn't help but chuckle before I introduced myself. I simply had to find out the story behind this mystery man.

His name was Ben, and he served as an elder of an older, more established church that had been trying to make changes to reach more people for Christ. He had heard about the growth of Real Life Ministries and wanted to see it for himself. As I could tell from his voice memos, Ben was deeply impacted by our church culture as we welcomed him and interacted with him. Our actions caused him to truly believe we had trained every third person in our church to be a greeter! I made sure to tell him that was *not the case* but instead that we had built a culture in which people naturally take ownership of their faith. That ownership translates into a lobby filled with people who live out the mission of Christ. He continued to comment on the love and transparency he felt from people he had never before met. Within minutes of entering our church building, God had impacted Ben and began opening his eyes to something different—to the relational environment that makes a healthy disciple-making culture grow.

Training up a greeting team is important and should be done. Our training supports and builds up culture. Our greeting teams are part of the strategy we live out. Yet our strategies should never replace culture. Creating a culture that sees each person who walks through the door as someone who should be noticed, loved, and welcomed, regardless of outward appearance, requires intentionality. This type of culture must be cultivated so that we can live our values in the fun and easy times, like a Sunday morning in the church lobby, as well as in the hard times when life gets painful.

Walking Through Painful Experiences

Two and half years have passed at the time of writing this book since my daughters were in a terrible car accident. Both survived the accident but suffered extensive injuries. My oldest daughter, Emma, suffered physical injuries, but more painful was her emotional trauma. She remembered every moment of the wreck, and the memories wreaked havoc on her. Olivia, my younger daughter, experienced extensive skull fractures, bleeding in the brain, and a double compound jaw fracture. She spent weeks in a coma, and only by the grace of God is she alive today. Olivia missed an entire year of school, which she had to take again the next year. She also missed a year of softball due to the accident, but her unwavering commitment through many months of difficult and painful rehab and gut-wrenching hard work earned her a spot on the high school varsity softball team for her (second) freshman year. If it wasn't for the relational nature of our church, I don't know how we would have made it through that traumatic experience. If we had cultivated a non-relational, information-focused culture, I may have walked away from ministry, or done something worse.

Even just recently, I remembered how thankful I was—and still am—for our relational church culture: In my current men's small group, I was sharing with some of the men about how painful that experience was for me as a parent. Even more than two years later, tears rolled down my cheeks as I confessed my deep fears of my daughter dying and the helpless feeling of trying to help both my daughters through that difficult time. I still struggle to articulate how my faith faltered at times during that season, yet God also showed incredible grace to me and my family. Sharing life like that requires feeling a certain amount of safety, and as a pastor, I have the same temptations as anyone else *not to share* what's really going on. But I do share because our church has a culture of relational safety.

After I shared with my group, one of the other men followed suit. He opened up and began to share about how he also struggled in his past with trusting God. He shared about the horrible abuse he went through as a child and how angry he had been at God. In a group of men, we were able to sit together and pour out our hurts. The environment of our group was safe, and he trusted that he could share things that had lain dormant in his heart and mind for years.

I felt the same way. Even though I had shared my struggles before, it felt just as vulnerable that day and that's how it feels every time I share them. Creating this type of environment doesn't automatically happen; it takes effort and time from intentional leaders, and this environment is a vital part of disciple-making culture.

The Two Pillars of a Biblical Relational Environment

Jesus intentionally created an environment in which those around him could talk through their struggles. Why do you think he was invited to so many parties with "sinners"? Think also of the many times the disciples opened up and asked questions or voiced their frustrations (e.g., Luke 8:9; Mark 9:9–13; Matt. 24:3). Consider how the woman at the well from John 4 felt around Jesus. I imagine her fighting back tears as she wrestled with her sin before Jesus. But Jesus demonstrated grace to her. Can you imagine the joy in her heart and the look in her eyes when she experienced true salvation?

In order to build a culture of biblical disciple-making, we must embrace the vital need to create safe environments for people. We know that the world can be a harsh, judgmental, and brutal place. So unfortunately, when people come into the church, they sometimes expect this sort of environment. When we look at the life of Christ, we see how Jesus created a relationally safe environment. He spoke truth—

> *We must embrace the vital need to create safe environments for people.*

which might have felt "harsh" to some people—but he also spoke grace. He knew when to push and when to provide space. Because of his leadership, his disciples walked in a culture of both truth *and* safety, which are the two pillars of a biblical relational environment. Safety helps people authentically express who they are, and truth challenges people to grow in their faith. This balance is difficult to create, but having both is essential if you want to experience the transformative power of making disciples at your church.

Pillar 1: A Safe Environment

We must weave into the tapestry of our disciple-making culture an environment where people feel safe. This comes through transparency and honesty, which helps people process life's greatest hurts, lies, insecurities, and failures. Then, and only then, can they experience the truth that sets them free. That environment will not become an essential part of your culture, however, unless you intentionally create it.

I recently sat with a good friend of mine who currently pastors a 120-year-old church. He claims that several of the founding members of the church still hold positions on the steering committee. While he jokes about this, that's at least how he feels sometimes! Over the last two years now he has diligently worked to change the culture from a traditional Sunday school model to an intentionally discipleship-focused model, which is more holistic. He began to express some of his frustration at his church's lack of change. They had shifted over fifty percent of the congregation to meeting in small groups which gathered in homes rather than in classrooms. Yet when he went to inspect how the groups were doing, he saw that group members still had surface-level relationships with one another, and they had neither the opportunity nor the inclination to openly share their lives and their concerns with one another in that setting. Meeting in homes did not automatically make people feel safe enough to discuss their struggles. Their church culture felt stuck, and discouragement was creeping into my friend's heart.

My heart ached for him because I, too, have had those moments when I felt stuck and could not seem to create the forward movement I had hoped to see in those I was leading. Out of compassion, I pressed him to describe the groups and what was happening in the homes. He perked up and began describing exactly how each group was going. The more he spoke, though, the deeper his brow furrowed and the more I could see frustration sweep across his face. He realized something as he listened to himself describe the groups. The teachers had exchanged the classroom lectern for the living room coffee table, but that hadn't changed their culture. They still lacked transparency and authenticity, and as a result, people were not growing in their relationships and neither were they growing in their application of the Word. Even though they were meeting in homes, they still had not created an intentional relational environment where people felt safe to share their hurts and struggles. They could not process without fear or shame how to apply God's Word to what they were experiencing. They had simply changed the scenery. Changing scenery doesn't change culture; only intentional leadership changes culture. And intentional leaders create safe, relational environments.

This story represents a common mistake: making merely cosmetic changes when the issue goes deeper—to the level of culture. Oftentimes, churches make the mistake of setting their crosshairs on "small groups," believing that if they start small groups, then they will automatically make disciples, and community will suddenly appear. I believe a living room can be a more conducive environment for disciple-making and community building, but it does not guarantee those outcomes. In fact, when small groups are done poorly you can end up inoculating your people against a more relational environment, which accomplishes the opposite effect you want. So remember that small groups are *not* the goal. Cultivating strong, spiritually healthy disciples who can make disciples is the goal. The environment where disciples are best made is a safe environment where people trust that their story will be heard respectfully and handled carefully and confidentially. This is what we call an intentional relational environment.

Cultivating strong,
spiritually healthy
disciples who can
make disciples
is the goal.

My pastor friend had set his sights on the wrong target. He thought if he just moved people into small groups, then *poof,* disciples would be made. He had unknowingly set the wrong goal. We will unpack exactly what a safe, healthy relational environment looks like below, but first I must say something about the truth side of the relational environment, the second pillar, before you declare me a heretic and think I do not care about teaching the Bible! I want to be clear that biblical truth is equally as vital to a healthy culture as safety is.

Pillar 2: A Truth-Filled Environment

We need biblical teaching, which means leaders need to equip people to understand the truths of Scripture and apply those truths to their lives. Jesus did this as he journeyed with his disciples: He taught, modeled, and lived out truth. He gave the disciples handles to grab ahold of truth and then live it out. He didn't just speak truth to change their belief systems, though; he created an environment that allowed them *to process the truth.* So when I emphasize creating a relational environment, I'm not downplaying the truth side at all. I'm actually saying that *in order for people to embrace the truths of the gospel and grow as believers, we must create the right environment.* Just like plants need air, water, nutrients, space, and time to grow, so does a disciple-making culture need the right ingredients to grow.

Going back to my pastor friend who had recently shifted his church toward small groups: I sat with him as we went back to the truths of Scripture and how his church needed to change some critical elements of their groups if they wanted to experience biblical discipleship. They had the truth part; they just needed to tweak the environment part. He began by shifting the goal of their small groups, which helped the overall culture of the groups. He did this by helping the leaders understand that the goal was not merely transferring information but living life together as they followed

God and raised up other disciple-makers. Their groups were slowly transformed, and people felt empowered to step up and participate in the mission of disciple-making. Yes, they taught biblical truth, but now they also had a relational environment, which helped them move from just the head truths to the truths in their hearts and hands as well.

Remember the man in my small men's group who opened up and shared about his hurts toward God? I, filling the role of the intentional leader, created that environment because I first modeled transparency. As I opened up and honestly shared my life, he felt like he could open up and share his too. Over the coming weeks, our group shared with him the truths of Scripture. We dove deep into the realities of the gospel and God's love for him. He heard it, received it, and eventually gave his life to Christ. Today, that man is apprenticing under a small group leader and preparing to disciple his own group one day. He saw truth lived out in a safe environment and experienced a culture that promoted the application of biblical truth.

Creating Your Small Group Guidelines

So how exactly do we create this type of environment where people feel safe and also experience the challenge of truth? First, I must say that the Holy Spirit was the one who moved in the hearts of both my pastor friend and the man in my small group. They experienced a culture cultivated by the Spirit that promoted healthy relationship. But catch this: the Spirit works through leaders who are greatly intentional and committed to sticking close to people through hard and even confusing times. That is how you will see this culture come to life. It's not always easy, and it's sometimes painful, but it's always worth it. I can't tell you how thankful I am that, as the lead pastor of my church, I could receive from my people in my time of need what I had taught them to give: living life together in love. When you create this relational environment that I'm describing, you see lives change and people experience the gospel in a powerful way.

We've introduced the two pillars of safety and truth. Now, let's put some flesh on those bones so you can implement in your context what I'm describing here. Our small groups at Real Life Ministries Texas use what we call "guidelines" to help us create our intentional environment. I would strongly encourage you to use ours, build a similar list, or even add to what I am giving you in the list below. Whatever you do, remember that what is not intentional is not reproducible. To build a culture of biblical disciple-making in your church, you must create healthy relational environments.

In our small groups, the leader (or sometimes the apprentice) communicates the guidelines at the beginning of each small group time. Sometimes the leader will ask group members to participate by sharing a guideline they recall. We use the following guidelines, each of which I will explain in turn below: confidentiality, don't rescue and don't fix, no crosstalk, use humor responsibly, give everyone a chance to share, use "I statements," and fight for relationship. What follows is the meaning of each of these terms. I've written these directed to group participants so you can use them to train your groups:

1. Confidentiality. Keep what is shared in the group confidential. This builds trust and places value on the person sharing. Confidentiality prevents gossip. As a group, we agree that what is said in the group stays in the group. This helps people feel like they can share what's really going on without being afraid it will "get out" to the wrong person.

2. Don't rescue and don't fix. When someone is sharing something deeply personal or painful, there can be a tendency to immediately try to make them feel better about themselves or the situation. But this often causes the person to stop sharing. In fact, this often results in the individual not going as deep as they might have gone.

How can we prevent this? Resist the temptation to "rescue" people. This means, instead of rescuing, listening to what people are sharing without trying to get them out of the spot they're in. It means listening without fixing them. If someone wants advice, let them ask for it. There can be a time to talk further, but inside the group is not that time. We strongly hold to the belief that it is not our job to fix each other; the Holy Spirit does that work. We are there to empathize, care for, and when appropriate, point people to Jesus and the Word of God.

3. No crosstalk. "Crosstalk" is when people talk over each other. So "no crosstalk" means that we are considerate of others as they share. Don't have side conversations while others are talking. When everyone feels like they are being listened to and heard by the entire group, this builds trust. Treat others in the group as you would want to be treated—by listening to them. *Note to the reader: You might think this is a given, but in my experience, it needs to be stated in groups in order to cultivate a culture of consideration like I'm describing here.*

4. Use humor responsibly. Fun is an essential part of small groups. When meeting in small group, however, keep sarcastic comments, jokes, and laughter to a minimum to allow for an atmosphere of authenticity and vulnerability. Nothing can kill the safety of a group more quickly than someone telling an inappropriate joke or making light of a situation that someone else might view as deeply personal.

5. Give everyone a chance to share. Whoever is facilitating the small group needs to create an environment where people are sensitive to the amount of time they spend sharing. A positive way of doing this is to encourage *every person* to participate in group discussions. If one person speaks the entire time, others may not engage or may not even return to the group. Asking someone else to share or kindly asking a person taking too much time talking to hold a thought creates an environment where everyone can participate.

6. Use "I statements." An "I statement" is when someone contributes to a conversation using "I" to describe their perspective instead of talking in generalized terms. We want to hear each group member's personal thoughts and perspectives, and when everyone uses "I statements" to answer discussion questions, it allows them to speak for themselves rather than generalizing by using terms such as "them," "the church," "us," or "we." This contributes to a relationally healthy environment where people are vulnerable and transparent too.

7. Fight for relationship. Relationship reaches a whole new level when we resolve conflicts in a healthy manner. When conflicts or sin issues arise between group members, commit to "fight" for the relationship. This means not hiding from conflict or disagreements but discussing them openly and in a healthy way. In a loving, kind, and honest way, encourage group members to work through their differences. We help people work toward resolution rather than abandon the relationship or give up for fear of conflict. This final guideline is so important, by the way, that I've devoted the whole next chapter to it.

You may use this list, a different set of guidelines, or develop a totally new list. Whatever you decide, I recommend keeping your list simple and short enough for everyone to remember it without using notes. That will help it to be memorable, which will lead to better implementation. I recommend you use no more than ten guidelines. Remember that these intentional guidelines help build a relational environment. This will not happen by accident, and most people have never walked out their own Christian journey in a healthy, safe environment. You have the opportunity to provide that for them.

Transformational Relationships

I am so thankful for the men and women with whom I have shared life in small groups. When our girls were in the car accident I mentioned above, it was the place where we found healing. On the days that I could not see through the pain and doubt, people sat with us, and families prayed with us. Together we sought the truth of Scripture, which served as a light in some pretty dark times in my life.

A church culture that upholds healthy relational environments will facilitate life change and move its culture from one of *transferring information* to *transforming lives*. The gospel is not about information transfer alone but about powerful transformation of the whole person. We see this lived out when we intentionally create relational environments. I encourage you to pay close attention to the culture you are creating at your church. What changes need to be made when people enter your culture? For example, when a new person walks into your lobby on Sunday morning, a new couple visits a small group, or a new volunteer joins a ministry, do newcomers feel welcomed? Do the regular folks linger around after gatherings, wanting to spend more time together in relationship? Do they invite others to join them for their fellowship time?

Probably more than any other concept in this book, I want you to understand one important fact about creating a disciple-making culture, and it's worth repeating: it starts with you! This is especially true for creating a relational environment because the way we do relationships is so second nature. More is caught than taught, and that's especially true with creating a disciple-making culture in which relationships feel safe and are saturated with truth. This sort of culture will come out of what you personally value and demonstrate. Whether in your home, ministry, or church, disciple-making culture comes from you and those in whom you make a life-on-life investment. This is not always easy; however, once you create this type of environment, you've got to fight to keep it going strong. In the next chapter, I share with you why this matters so much and what it looks like on a practical, church-wide level.

Small Group Guidelines for a Healthy Culture

As you begin to apply boundaries and guidelines to your church's small group culture, I encourage you to visit **himpublications.com/culture** to download a sample list of the group guidelines we use at our church called "Small Group Guidelines for a Healthy Culture." Nothing destroys a relational environment more quickly than a breach of confidentiality. How does this happen? Small groups that lack clear guidelines can do more damage than good when it comes to church culture. The health of your relational environments will directly determine the effectiveness of your culture in producing disciple-makers. So download and print off this list of guidelines. Use them as a starting point to form guidelines that work for your church. You might add a few of your own or write an entirely new list. Whatever you do, remember that every relational environment needs basic guidelines to ensure a consistent and healthy culture in which everyone feels safe. You as the intentional leader must create this type of culture! Visit our additional resource page at **himpublications.com/culture** and download this sample of small group guidelines.

9

FIGHT FOR IT

*Fight for relationships by resolving
conflict in a biblical way.*

Let's face it, relationships are hard work. The Scriptures are filled with examples of how sin destroys relationships. We also know from Scripture that the sacrificial act of Jesus on the cross restored our relationships with God and one another in Christ. This was part of God's "fight" for relationship with us. Since the Garden of Eden, humankind has struggled with relationships. The truth is that all relationships—marriage relationships, sibling relationships, friendships, you name it—take work. In today's world, very few are willing to do this hard work. In fact, Western culture as a whole often promotes and even celebrates leaving a relationship when it gets hard. Contrary to the world's message and cultural example, the truth of Scripture promotes something very different. In Christ, we are called to work through our differences, forgive one another, show grace to each other, and fight for our relationships. Unfortunately, in the church today very few people know how to fight for relationships. Instead, we're skilled at avoiding conflict. Past hurts and experiences weigh us down, as if they were heavy rocks we carry around in a backpack.

The Need for Healthy Conflict

I dislike conflict as much as the next person, but I have learned that when I avoid it, nothing gets resolved and the relationship is eventually doomed—unless I fight for it. To fight for a relationship might seem counterintuitive to you. To many, the word "fight" means yelling and screaming, or throwing insults and using belittling language. But fights do not have to be like that, not at all. When I teach people to "fight for it," I mean that we press in and truly seek to resolve whatever issue is at hand. We value the person and our relationship with them more than our own pride. In the church today, however, Christians often avoid issues or the person with whom they have an issue, or even worse, they quit going to the church where the conflict took place. When they leave a church, they often justify it by saying things like, "God has called us away from that church." Or I hear people say (and I love this one), "I just want to be *grace-filled*, so I don't want to confront that person who upset me." But biblically we are called to press in and love one another *by working though our differences.* This means that sometimes we even confront others in a loving way.

> We are called to press in and love one another by working though our differences.

I have heard it said that "hurt people hurt people." Each of us carries with us some relational hurt from the past. People hurt each other, often unintentionally, as a result of our own woundedness. In today's church environment, where conflict and relational hurt occurs, we rarely face these issues head on. Rather than dealing with conflict in a godly way and fighting for relationships, we give up. We quit. I am not saying anyone should stay in an

Fight for
relationships.

unbiblical or abusive church; I am saying we must resist the urge to stuff our hurts into a backpack of burdens. We must tuck away our insecurities and have the courage to *fight for relationships*. We set a different kind of example when we roll up our sleeves and resolve issues—when we keep a light backpack, you could say. This example comes when we allow the Holy Spirit to work in us and build a culture where we value and fight for relationships.

To understand the Lord's heart for community, we must read Jesus' prayer in John 17:20–21 about unity: "My prayer is not for them alone. I pray also for those who will believe in me through their message, that all of them may be one, Father, just as you are in me and I am in you. May they also be in us so that the world may believe that you have sent me."

He says that if we become one as he and the Father are one, then the whole world will come to know him. Did you catch that? He says *the whole world!* That means our greatest evangelistic tool is not the latest outreach program. Instead, our effectiveness in reaching the lost depends on our ability to stay unified. Remaining unified implies that we must maintain unity. Maintaining unity means that we fight for relationships and do all we can to avoid disunity. *The root of disunity is a breakdown of relationships!*

Living It Out

Let me share with you an example of what this looks like. Scott, a man from my small group, stopped coming to our group. So I called him to find out why. The reasons he gave me were pretty weak for a guy who used to be really passionate about our group and almost never missed a meeting. I immediately knew something else was going on. You see, it's in moments like this when we, as disciple-makers, have a choice to make: *Do we fight for relationship, culture, and a healthy environment, or do we accept answers like this and avoid the conflict?* I had to decide, and I chose to fight through it.

Here's how I did it: I called Scott and asked him to meet me for coffee. We met in a coffee shop, and after the normal greetings and catching up, I looked him in the eye and asked him directly, "So, what's going on?" Immediately, he hung his head, shifted in his seat several times, and then looked up at me. He began to describe to me how Bill, another guy in our group, had hurt him. Bill's comments to Scott about a life issue after group were a bit harsh, and Scott took his words very hard. What seemed very simple and innocent to one person, deeply wounded another.

I sat with Scott and listened to his story. I learned more about his past and the difficulties he had worked through. Scott began to unload his hurts and fears. After two hours of discussion, Scott had moved from wanting to leave our group, and possibly leave the church, to feeling like he was loved and part of something special. I encouraged Scott to sit down with Bill and share his heart. I knew that while our conversation was a good first step, Scott needed to go to Bill in love and talk it out with him.

The amazing thing is that Scott did just that! I will never forget the call I got after the guys had their meeting. Scott was like a new man. He told me it was the first time he could remember in his adult life that he sat across the table from another man and worked through a conflict. In the past he had avoided it, or worse, tried to ignore it. He told me, "Brandon, for the first time I feel like I'm walking in freedom."

Jesus tells us in Matthew 5:24 that if we have an issue with a brother, we need to leave our sacrifice at the altar and go make things right: "Leave your gift there before the altar and go. First be reconciled to your brother, and then come and offer your gift" (ESV). He also tells us that are we are called not just to love God but also our neighbor (Matt. 22:37–38). How in the world can we ever love a fellow brother or sister in Christ if we are not willing to fight through conflict with them? And it is not an issue of *whether or not* we will have conflict; it is a matter of *when* we will have it. Conflict is part of being human, and biblically speaking, we are called to work through it. When we put in the hard work of resolving conflict, we bring glory to God and work toward unity.

Get Started and Be Proactive

I ask my staff on a weekly basis, "Is everyone doing well relationally?" Then, as a group, we allow each person to process whether there is any conflict or hurt among us. At Real Life Ministries Texas, we established this authentic engagement from the start. It is a common practice for us, yet some weeks this practice still requires uncommon courage.

If this practice of asking how people are doing relationally is new in your church culture, you as a leader need to model how to answer this question by going first. A general principle of small groups is that the group will only go as deep as the leader is willing to go, and that is true for working through conflict as well. It may take time to develop trust in each other, so we must be proactive and not allow the sun to go down on our anger. We have a responsibility to create a culture where we can process our hurts and frustrations.

Sometimes we need to go one-on-one to the person with whom we have an issue because the issue might be more private and not appropriate to discuss in a larger group. Regardless of how conflict is addressed—in a group setting or one-on-one—we must build a culture that promotes conflict resolution. We can only build and maintain relational environments if we are willing to do the hard work.

Principles for Healthy Fighting

I have listed below three key principles that I use for fighting for relationships in a healthy way:

1. Seek first to resolve a conflict one-on-one. Few things are more embarrassing or frustrating than being confronted by someone in front of a group of people. When there is an issue between two people, it is always best for them to try and resolve it one-on-one first. Matthew 18:15–20 tells us that when there is a sin issue, the first step is to go alone to the person who sinned to confront them about it. You should follow this relational principle to help promote healthy culture. If two people cannot resolve their issue one-on-one, then it's time to bring in someone else (also from Matthew 18).

2. Ask clarifying questions at the start of a conflict. Often hurts that cause conflict arise from miscommunication. The devil loves to work his way into these situations and twist words. So practice sincerely asking clarifying questions and encouraging others to do this to better understand a situation before arriving at conclusions. Frequently, when I need to confront someone, I will ask, "If I am hearing you correctly, you are saying . . . . Am I hearing you right?" I do this to make sure I am not misunderstanding or taking something personally that was not intended to be taken that way. This helps to provide clarity and remove guesswork from the equation. As a result, this helps avoid unnecessary conflicts. When there is an offense, clarifying questions can help the other person feel understood and not feel attacked.

3. Own your part of the issue. Many of us forget that in conflict there are two parties. It's sometimes easier for us to see the other person's part in the issue. Looking in the mirror and seeing our part can be difficult, or even painful. When we build trust with others, we can receive a person's frustration and open the door for them to confront or challenge us in an area we might be hurting them. We need to be humbly open to this feedback and know it will help us understand the situation better. In this way, we create a culture in which confrontation is not threatening or frightening because each person humbly admits their fault when appropriate.

Our Debt to One Another

Let's take this concept of fighting for relationships a bit deeper now. In Romans 13:8, Paul writes these profound words about relationships: "Let no debt remain outstanding, except the continuing debt to love one another, for he who loves his fellow man has fulfilled the law."

Through these words, the Holy Spirit reminds us that we live in a *continuing debt* to love one another! We have a debt to love each other that can never be completely met. The debt of love among us as people is one that we should always try to pay back. When we understand the incredible debt that Christ has paid for us, then we can understand what we owe him—our love. We live this love out not just by loving him but also by loving people. This love should propel us to fight for relationships. We work out our debt to love each other without conditions, especially when we are in conflict.

Imagine if churches did everything they could to live out this principle within the confines of their own body of believers. How incredibly attractive would that be to a lost and dying world? What if leaders in our churches fought for relationships by trying to pay back the debt to love each other? What would happen if we focused on standing on biblical truth and fighting for relationships rather than fighting about stuff, equipment, and the color of the carpet? I suspect we would experience unity, and the world would witness us actually living out the gospel. I had a great opportunity to experience this exact challenge with my own staff.

Healthy Conflict with Your Leaders Too

Several years ago, one of my friends and I had a conflict. She was frustrated with some things that I had said and felt like I wasn't treating her fairly. We were working together on a project at our church, and I unintentionally hurt her feelings. She asked me if we could meet together. During this meeting, while she fidgeted in her chair, she opened up to me and began describing what was going on with her, starting with some negative experiences with church leaders from her past. Years before, she had served in a church where leaders avoided confrontation. In fact, conflict was a ticket for being removed from your position of serving at the church. Anyone who tried to confront an issue or dysfunctional behavior was ridiculed and their point was minimized. That told me she had served in an unhealthy culture. In a culture like that, it is impossible to carry out any of the three key principles of fighting for relationships I listed above.

I had unintentionally offended her, and we had to sit down and work through the issues she brought up. I fought the desire to be defensive, and together we fought for the relationship. Within an hour, we came to a mutual understanding and worked out our differences. She was able to move beyond her past hurts, and we established for her a new norm of church culture. She was now able to handle future issues with peace and confidence because we established in our church culture that healthy conflict was not only okay but also essential for relationships to flourish. She now coaches other staff and volunteers in her ministry to effectively resolve conflict.

Think about this for a moment: when the leaders of her previous church might have hurt or offended one of the staff members, the offended person did not feel they had the freedom to discuss it with them *without the risk of being fired* or removed from a volunteer position. This is terrible, yet common! I am not suggesting that every church has a culture like this. What I am trying to point out is that more often than not, we build cultures in the church that look more like a business of employees than a church of family members. To build a healthy culture, we as leaders must start with us, no matter our level of leadership—even at the top—and be willing to work through conflict and hurt. This enables us to create healthy relational environments where people walk with security and freedom.

When the woman at our church came to me, she was still afraid she might lose not only her position, which she loved and felt called by God to do, but also the friendship we had forged over several years of working alongside one another. Her tears flowed. Because of her past, she was uncertain of the ramifications of a confrontation in the present. When she surfaced the issue, though, I praised her for being honest and having the courage to talk it out. We easily talked through her frustration, and I apologized and owned my part in the situation. Together we overcame the issues at hand, and almost immediately, a lightness returned to our relationship and a deeper trust was built.

On the Flip Side

Now imagine for a moment that we did not have that reconciling conversation, and she nurtured fear and bitterness toward me. People sense that stuff in a person. I know what would have happened because I see it all the time in churches: A fakeness or lack of genuine love would follow. Because of how small we were and how central a role this person played in our budding new church, if friction remained between us, church members would have quickly recognized that I did not live by the standards I was teaching. Few, if any, would have stuck with us amid that kind of hypocrisy, and the church would have struggled to even get off the ground.

Thankfully, I have seen the willingness of staff members, elders, and key volunteers to do the hard work of fighting for relationship. This leads to healthy outcomes like the one I described with Scott and Bill. Thriving disciples are immersed in relational environments that convey, "We will fight for relationships." What this really says to people is that we will fight for *you!* What better way exists to build a culture of Christlike love than to fight for someone like that? We must have the courage to examine ourselves and be willing to remove the rocks we have in our backpacks in order to create a culture where people can come to each other and have the necessary conversations to work out their differences. That culture will display unity: not perfect unity but a unity that at least moves toward the unity Jesus talks about in John 17.

I want to say again that building a culture in which people can discuss frustration and hurt takes work and commitment toward paying the debt of loving each other. This is some of the most difficult and exhausting work we can do in the church. I wish I could say that every situation turns out well and that we always have a big group hug afterwards, but that doesn't always happen. I will tell you, though, that relationships in the body of Christ are worth fighting for regardless of the outcome, because we are commanded to be in unified relationships. Jesus died so that we can live in good relationships with him and one another. Our relationships with each other are never perfect because they involve *people*, but they are worth fighting for—no matter what. Now, as we continue to look at the relational environment that is so vital to disciple-making culture, consider how modeling this authentic, relational community can help you build, and even shift, the culture of your church.

10

MODEL IT

Model authentic, relational community.

We live in a world that is moving at a breakneck speed, which is the number one barrier keeping churches from developing a relationally authentic disciple-making culture. For leaders, between our families, careers, ministry commitments, and hopefully finding time to have fun, it doesn't seem like there is time to make disciples the way Jesus did. Life feels like it's moving faster all the time, and you probably feel the tension of wanting to make disciples but also wondering how that fits into your schedule.

I totally understand this feeling. I hear people all the time say, "Jesus lived at a different pace than we do today; I don't have time to make disciples like he did." I used to think that way too, but after more than twenty years of doing my best to live out a disciple-making lifestyle, I believe this mentality is misguided. Granted, Jesus didn't live in a world of high-speed internet, technology overload, convenient global travel, and the overall busyness in which we sometimes get caught. We are at a disadvantage because we have less time to spend investing into people.

Or do we?

How we choose to spend our time determines how our church culture develops. Relationships take time, and cultivating discipling relationships among our church family requires the same intentionality and time as any other relationship. Slowing down and modeling for someone what following Jesus looks like and cultivating a culture of disciple-making has become a fading art. It's like the time it takes to learn the art of fly fishing.

The Time to Teach, the Time to Learn

Teaching someone to fly fish requires modeling and an investment of time. When I first learned to fly fish, I stayed in close proximity to my instructor, watching every move he made: his casting with its smooth, fluid motion, his placing the fly in the right place on the river, and how he properly set the hook. This all requires time and practice. One of my great joys thus far in life has been passing on the art of fly fishing to my sons.

I watched my son Garrett strip line through his hand. He was fighting the beautiful cutthroat trout he had just hooked on his fly rod as he stood knee-deep in the St. Joe River (in Idaho). For several months prior to that day, Garrett, Grady, and I practiced fly fishing in our back yard. Cast after cast, repeating and practicing— they learned. Each time we practiced, their motions became more fluid as they more closely imitated me. Practicing the rhythmic and consistent motions of fly fishing is the only way to learn—and to avoid a knotted mess in your line. My boys would watch me, then do. They asked "why" questions about certain motions and "what if" questions about potential problems. As I took the time to model fly fishing for them, they learned, and that led to the day both of my boys—Grady and Garrett—landed their first trout on a fly rod.

Watching them fight the fish was rewarding for me as they alternated between looking awkward and looking as if they had done this a hundred times. I could see small motions that felt like looking at myself in a mirror, yet it was them doing it. They improvised and made adaptations to what I had taught them, repeating a beautiful process that I had modeled for them. That day of fishing was successful not just because we caught fish but also because they had learned to fish. I sat back, watched, and celebrated their success.

Life-on-Life, Relational Disciple-Making

The Gospels show us how Jesus intentionally modeled relational disciple-making. Think about the life-on-life conversations he had with the people as he sat on hillsides. Through these conversations, he taught them. Others followed him as he traveled from town to town. Many of these people wanted to be healed or to witness a miracle. They were primarily observers in a crowd as they experienced Jesus, but for those who were constantly with Jesus, they had an all-access pass to the life of Jesus. They ate with him, laughed around campfires with him, and walked along roads with him.

Jesus didn't sidestep the relational aspect of disciple-making; he embraced it as essential to his ministry. Why did Jesus work so diligently to create a culture of relational environments? Because he wasn't content with his disciples, especially the Twelve, knowing about him in some sort of vacuum. He wanted more for them. James tells us that even the demons have knowledge of God, but their knowledge doesn't result in their surrendering to him (Jam. 2:19). Jesus never wanted his followers to understand his teachings so that they could simply raise their theological pedigree. He sought true transformation, which comes primarily through life-on-life relationships.

We live in a church culture today that emphasizes biblical knowledge but undervalues relational maturity. What does it actually look like to follow Jesus, to be changed by what we know about him, and to be on mission with the one about whom we have all that information? Jesus was consumed with modeling for his disciples what it meant to share in his life. He wanted them to know him *by being with him*, and that modeling was foundational to the culture he created. We see in the New Testament not only how Jesus modeled this but also how the early church modeled this for future generations of believers.

What Jesus Modeled, His Disciples Lived Out

On the day of Pentecost—after Jesus was resurrected and had ascended to heaven—the disciples were gathered together in one room (Acts 2). Notice that they weren't in their own homes praying separately but together! That's when the Holy Spirit made his entrance onto the scene. Scripture says the Spirit entered the room with a sound like a violent wind and rested on the disciples like tongues of fire. The disciples were empowered by God to speak in different tongues from their native language, and their sound drew a large crowd.

Peter stood up and began proclaiming the gospel of Jesus. The discipleship journey begins when one person boldly proclaims the gospel and someone else receives it, but the story does not end there! Here's how Pentecost ended: After a powerful message by Peter, many other people were "cut to the heart" (v. 37) and asked what they had to do to be saved. Peter instructed them to repent and be baptized. At this point, 3,000 people turned to Jesus for salvation and followed Peter's instructions. The gospel was boldly proclaimed, and the church was born.

The story continues as Luke, the author of Acts, describes the relational environment of the early church: "They devoted themselves to the apostles' teaching and to the fellowship, to the breaking of bread and to prayer" (Acts 2:42). Unfortunately, too many churches have stopped the discipleship process at conversion, and they don't always take it to the fellowship of believers. But making a decision to follow Jesus is only the beginning of a disciple's journey!

Thankfully, Peter and the other disciples had watched Jesus model authentic, relational community for the purpose of life-long discipleship. That's why, following the conversion of thousands in Acts 2, the disciples invited the new believers into the same type of community they had experienced with Jesus, for the purpose of making disciples who make disciples. This is what we find in Acts 2, which I began to quote above. Read the rest of this account of the earliest relational church culture on record, and you will see Jesus' method of disciple-making put into action by the men and women in whom he had invested three years of his life. Notice the relational elements of this passage (*in italics*):

> They devoted themselves to the apostles' teaching and *to the fellowship*, to the breaking of bread and to prayer. Everyone was filled with awe, and many wonders and miraculous signs were done by the apostles. All the believers *were together* and *had everything in common*. Selling their possessions and goods, they *gave to anyone as he had need. Every day they continued to meet together* in the temple courts. They broke bread *in their homes* and *ate together* with glad and sincere hearts, praising God and *enjoying the favor of all the people.* (Acts 2:42–47)

The disciples who led the early church did exactly what Jesus had done: they lived their disciple-making journey in the context of everyday life. After conversion, people began to devote themselves to the apostles' teaching. They attended church, but they also spent time in fellowship with one another. They ate meals in one another's homes, they got together for prayer, and they took care of one another's physical and financial needs. Discipleship, and disciple-making, happened in relational community which was led and modeled by the first followers

You cannot make a disciple of Jesus without cultivating a relational environment.

of Jesus. I will go as far as to say this: *You cannot make a disciple of Jesus without cultivating a relational environment.* To take it a step further: if you make disciples without relationship, they're not disciples of Jesus; they're disciples of you and your own model. The earliest followers of Jesus built his church with the methods Jesus used during his life and ministry. He had shown them what it looked like, and the early church carried on his relational culture. The results were staggering! The end of Acts 2:47 says, "And the Lord added to their number daily those who were being saved." The culture they carried on, empowered by the Holy Spirit, became the catalyst for the spread of the gospel to the farthest reaches of the earth.

Relational environments are just as important for the growth of the church today as they were in the early church. The more we disciple people in relational environments in our churches, the more people will invite their lost friends into a disciple-making culture where the love of Jesus is at work. His love will work its way into the hearts of those who are far from him. Christianity not only started in community but it also spreads most effectively in relational environments.

This Is How We Do It

Even in the Old Testament we see in relational terms the call to model what a life of following God looks like. In Deuteronomy 6, God gives clear instructions to parents about how to pass the truth of God on to their children. These verses, known as the *Shema* (which is Hebrew for the word "hear"), reveal the relational nature of disciple-making in the home:

> Hear, O Israel: The LORD our God, the LORD is one. Love
> the LORD your God with all your heart and with all your
> soul and with all your strength. These commandments that
> I give you today are to be upon your hearts. *Impress them on*

> *your children. Talk about them when you sit at home and when you walk along the road, when you lie down and when you get up. Tie them as symbols on your hands and bind them on your foreheads. Write them on the doorframes of your houses and on your gates.* (Deut. 6:4–9)

Did you notice all the life-on-life elements in this passage (*in italics*)? Parents have the responsibility of discipling their children in the greatest relational environment imaginable: the home! The same process of disciple-making Jesus used with his disciples finds its origin in the method of disciple-making God established in the old covenant. Pay close attention to the culture God implemented for the purpose of passing along faith from one generation to the next, because it happens in the context of relational environments through intentional modeling by parents to children.

Relational Disciple-Making: A Family Affair

A friend of mine has an eleven-year-old son who occasionally has night terrors that cause him a great deal of anxiety. My friend expressed how that could have caused major problems with their nightly routines and sleep patterns, but instead it has become an opportunity for him to see God at work. His little boy regularly fights anxiety by asking his dad to help him memorize a verse of Scripture to speak into his fears, or by asking his dad to pray over him so that he can be comforted by the awareness that Jesus is his refuge and shield.

The relationship my friend has developed with his son in their home has created a relational environment for disciple-making to occur, even in those troubling moments. It's their family culture, just the way they live life together. Where did his son learn to ask about or know that his dad could provide answers to his fears? His father modeled for him how to turn to Jesus and his Word when life becomes difficult. I've had the pleasure of spending several evenings with my friend as he interacts with his kids. I see how he allows his kids to see a strong, yet transparent, side of their dad. He consistently points them to Christ and shares his own dependency on Christ too.

Creating a relational family culture like that is just a small version of what it takes to create a relational culture in a church. Church is just one big family culture. As church leaders, we must model the methods of Jesus, and that requires authentic, relational environments. American culture today doesn't naturally allow for these sorts of environments. In fact, we live in an age where people have hundreds, if not thousands, of social media friends and followers but very few real-world relationships where friends know each other's hearts and souls. So we must fight hard to create a lifestyle of disciple-making built around deep, authentic relationships. This may mean we have to rethink our priorities and change our schedules in order to create margin to model for others a life they have never before seen.

Through the Relational Discipleship Network, of which I'm currently a member of the board, I have the opportunity to train pastors from around the United States and around the world, which is our main purpose as an organization.[5] Whether I am working with leaders in the U.S. or in foreign countries, the consistent feedback I hear from our training events is how much people learned from us *by watching us*. We create, as best we can, relational environments during our leadership trainings, so participants have an opportunity to get a small window into our real-life relationships. They often say that our training material was good, but watching us interact as a team *was inspiring*. They see us live out our values, and modeling those values puts real-life examples right in front of them. That's what a healthy disciple-making culture offers: real-life examples of real-life discipleship. When people see our culture lived out

Relationships
take time.

in the midst of biblical teaching, it hits home for them—because people need to see something in action in order to effectively apply it. Our job is not to change the whole world on our own, but together—by the power of the Holy Spirit, to the glory of God the Father, as we follow Jesus the Son—we can change the whole world, one person at a time.

Sacrifice Is Required

The hours I spent in the back yard modeling for my boys how to fly fish came at a price to me: time, which is a precious commodity for all of us. I chose to spend time with them rather than spending time doing something else. That's an important decision you will make one thousand times one thousand, but it's vital if you want to see your church culture shift toward becoming a disciple-making culture. Our staff spends time living life together the best we know how, which is still imperfect. We could do other things, but we choose this kind of commitment to each other, and we make sacrifices. Over time, when you and those around you choose relationship in this way, it simply becomes the way you function as a group. That's how culture works. Sacrifice is required to do things the Jesus way!

I regret none of the time I spend with my sons, especially in moments like when I saw my sons land their first trout. It might seem small but to me it was rewarding beyond words because it represents something bigger than fishing for trout: the relationship and growth we shared together. When we as church leaders see others begin to practice a life of following Jesus, because God used us to model that life, we start to really reach people. Nothing brings greater glory to God than when we learn to effectively fish for people. And it gets even better when those we've taught to fish for people then go on to teach others to do the same. That is better than landing any trout or going on any fishing trip. It's called the reproducible process of disciple-making. To this we now turn for our final key component.

Key Component 4

REPRODUCIBLE PROCESS

How to Reproduce a Disciple-Making Culture

11

TRAIN IT

*Develop a system that trains disciple-makers
to live out disciple-making culture.*

Three years into our new church plant, I stood in front of our staff, elders, small group leaders, and key volunteers—most of whom are now strong disciple-makers—and posed an important question to the group. This question came in the midst of my vision-casting about how God was going to use our group to change a community: "How many of you are leading a small group and discipling another person for the first time in your Christian life?" Hands shot up all over the room. I asked them to stand, and more than half the room stood. Emotion welled up in my heart and goosebumps covered my arms because I knew we were a part of something special: effectively expanding God's kingdom in a way that was reproducible.

On another level, a realization came over me that deepened my resolve to equip people to fulfill Jesus' command to go and make disciples. Before I tell you this realization, though, let me give you a little context. Just a few years prior, many of these disciple-makers were not even close to making disciples. In fact, some were not even believers. Most could not have even told you *what a disciple is*, let alone how to make one. If I had asked them, I'm sure they would have told you that disciple-making was something done by a Sunday School teacher, or even worse, it was the pastor's job. But that night, a fresh revelation hit me: disciple-making is not elusive. It's totally possible, by the grace and power of God, to create a process that works—repeatedly. I had seen it work in Idaho, and now I was seeing it work in a completely different context. Everyone in the room clearly understood that they were a disciple of Jesus who was committed to making disciples of Jesus.

> *Disciple-making is not elusive.*

Great Disciple-Makers Require Training

Greatness rarely, if ever, happens by accident. Hard work and training build a person into something great. Oftentimes, people like the idea of being great at something without putting in the work to get there. I will never forget when I was a kid, seeing a video of the famous Chicago Bears running back Walter Payton as he trained during the offseason. The cameraman stood at the top of a gigantic hill with a steep, arduous trail winding its way to the bottom. The video showed Payton sprinting up the trail, his legs and arms pounding as he pushed himself to conquer the hill. It was inspirational to watch his dedication to becoming great. After watching that video, it was easy to understand why he was so great at football.

Why would we not approach disciple-making with the desire to be great, knowing the hard work and consistency it takes? Unfortunately, we rarely call people to master the art of disciple-making, even though it's the core task of a mature disciple. Think of how short we fall when we *only* teach people to study Scripture. Disciple-making is so much more than teaching information. Disciple-makers must not just *know about* the truths of Scripture but they must also train disciples how to *live out* the truths of Scripture and put into practice the skills of disciple-making. Disciple-making requires great intentionality. When we examine the Gospels, we see Jesus preparing his disciples for this task. They may not have realized it, but Jesus was having them run up steep hills, navigate obstacles, and do everything else necessary to train for a commissioning that would eventually cost many of them their lives.

There is a big difference between book knowledge about how something works and the actual experience of knowing how to do something. When our disciple-makers at Real Life Ministries Texas stood up, I felt a deep sense of responsibility to prepare them and train them for what lay ahead. I am sure Walter Payton spent countless hours studying playbooks, but there is not enough mere head knowledge in the world to equip him to survive four quarters of an NFL football game. He had to put in the necessary training hours to implement what he knew. That's what disciple-makers must do as well.

In previous chapters, we talked about concepts like modeling, communicating, and living out disciple-making so that a culture of disciple-making permeates everything you do. To ensure that your church reproduces your culture on multiple levels, you must intentionally train them how to do that. *So how exactly do we train people to be reproducing disciple-makers?*

Laying Out a Plan

Before I dive into the details, I want to reiterate something critical: the natural instinct of many Christian leaders today is to think *how to program* disciple-making, but we need to think *how to train* disciple-making. Leaders often focus on the curriculum and how to systematize it. The problem with this is not the curriculum itself, which can certainly be a valuable component of following Jesus today. But

Disciple-making requires great intentionality.

I guarantee you that if you shift the focus from the programmatic to the relational, the effectiveness of what you are doing will increase. Even within the training itself, you and your team must continue to live out your values and the elements of your culture, or you risk your training being ineffective.

To help you avoid this risk, I offer five key principles to help you train your current and future disciple-makers. These principles are what we use at Real Life Ministries Texas, and they've proven effective time and time again:

1. Create a training plan. A training plan is your detailed plan for delivering instruction. Whether training people one-on-one or in small groups, you must establish a developed training plan that allows you to equip those who are leading, or will lead, in your disciple-making culture. As you start building a training plan, you must first determine what your people need to learn and apply. Oftentimes, churches build elaborate educational systems for volunteers and leaders without asking good questions of those who are about to be trained. Make sure to understand early on where the people you're training feel deficient or insecure with regard to disciple-making. Otherwise, you risk wasting everyone's time with good information that lacks the punch of giving exactly what they need. Here are some additional tips for creating your plan:

- Spend time with volunteers and ask them which areas they feel most insecure about when discipling others.
- Inspect the fruit of your church. Identify areas you see that need improvement (e.g., lack of facilitation skills, Bible literacy, inviting new families, relational maturity, etc.).
- Once you have inspected the fruit (or lack thereof), whiteboard those topics that will help you address areas for improvement. This can help you weave appropriate topics into your training, which improves the accuracy of your content

when helping your disciple-makers become more effective at making disciples.

- Structure your training program to begin with the simplest, most foundational information. Then, lead up to more advanced training. Skills and knowledge should build upon the initial foundational training.
- Pray and ask God to reveal what else they need.

A final thought for creating a plan: Remember that in this life we never "arrive." We'll always have areas that require more attention. So encourage those helping you train to remain humble and fight the "expert mentality," which believes that the goal is to arrive at a state of becoming the resident expert. Fighting this mentality promotes unity in the body by conveying that no one has truly arrived and that we all must continue to learn and grow. It also allows room for the more experienced disciple-makers to grow and for the less experienced disciple-makers to feel like they can engage as well.

2. Set the calendar. The church often finds itself "fitting into" the calendar created by the secular world. School dates, holidays, sports, and community events often determine how we build our church calendars. Here's how I've learned to handle that: Do your best to work with people's calendars but don't completely cater to them. Find the natural break times when your people are most likely to attend trainings, but these will probably still be inconvenient to some people—and that's okay. Disciple-making isn't supposed to be easy. Still give people plenty of notice and communicate dates early and as often as possible.

Also, I recommend that you hold training sessions for your disciple-makers at consistent times each year *and no more than three times a year.* We offer only two major trainings with our people each year (one in January and one in August). Expecting people at too many training events can cause burnout, and people will struggle with feeling like all they do is meet at the church. We ask much of our disciple-makers—staff and non-staff alike—so we want to hit a home run with the two training events we ask them to attend each year. That's why you must optimize your training calendar. Here are some extra tips on this point:

- Study school calendars to learn the critical dates for your area each year. Do not plan a summer training the week school starts or the week of graduation.
- Give yourself some space. Avoid major holidays and the week that kids go back to school. So, for example, if your training event is on a Saturday, do not plan other major church events that Sunday (avoid also the previous and following weekends). Also, fight the urge to plan trainings at the same time as other church events.
- Consider providing childcare so that when you host your training events, you maximize who is able to attend.
- Finally, schedule short training moments into your team, staff, and elder meetings. In our staff meetings at Real Life Ministries Texas, we schedule dedicated time for simple tips in specific areas that need attention. These are more informal but can be used to effectively invest into your teams.

Remember that building a culture of disciple-making is *who you are,* not *what you do,* so consistent investment into your core leaders is critical for your culture.

3. Use staff and non-staff disciple-makers at training events. Church members today often view staff as the professionals and volunteers as, well . . . just volunteers. We've got to change this if we're going to see a truly reproducible process implemented in our churches. Let's break down the "us versus them" mentality that separates the paid from the unpaid disciple-makers. This is important to culture-making, and there is no better place to do this than at your training events. Some of your best trainers might be volunteers who lead in obscure places in the church. Be willing to involve them in your training—or even allow them to facilitate the training! This too models an important aspect of biblical disciple-making culture. Even though you might be a paid staff person, training events are one of your greatest opportunities to empower those you lead and to give them a seat at the training table.

As you build this culture, you will be able to see competent leaders emerge. It also allows you to see who is lagging behind and needs a boost. So ask your most effective disciple-makers to pass on their skills and knowledge to others. This is not to say you cannot have staff lead trainings. Just think about what sort of culture you want to create. This kind of involvement from unpaid individuals increases buy-in and provides a hands-on opportunity for spiritual growth. Here are some suggestions that will help get volunteers involved in training events:

- Create opportunities for disciple-makers who have been equipped to train the next batch of disciple-makers.
- Provide multiple areas where volunteers can participate in training events to increase overall buy-in.
- When brainstorming in preparation for training events, ask the question, "Could a volunteer effectively do what a staff person is doing?" If the answer is yes, then ask a qualified volunteer to do it!

4. Set goals. You must determine if your training events are working. To do this, set goals and track whether or not they're being met. Set goals that are attainable and realistic for your church's current place along the journey. For example, your goal might be for all disciple-makers to complete the first training event and memorize your church's definition of a disciple. Or you might set a goal to have half your small group leaders bring an apprentice with them to the training, someone they are going to disciple and prepare to lead a new group in the coming months.

As you set goals, think about whom you want to help reach those goals. For example, if you want to train new apprentices, track them to see if the apprentices are forming and leading new small groups. Here are some tips for setting training goals:

- Discuss goals with your team and capture them on a whiteboard or somewhere you can go back to after the training. Once your training is completed, evaluate how well you did at accomplishing the goals.
- Share your goals with those being trained when appropriate.
- Create buy-in to what you are trying to accomplish.
- Build on your goals for the next training. For example, if you only had two new small group leaders at one training event, set a goal of doubling or tripling that number for the next one.

Intentionality is critical to effectively training the people in your church. If you don't intentionally set goals, it can be difficult to keep progressing. You can always adjust your training program based on how useful it is, so set a challenging target and have fun chasing it down.

5. Celebrate the wins. When we first planted our church, several of my team members challenged me to celebrate more. My tendency once we accomplish a goal is to simply move on to the next goal, but they were right to challenge me on this. Now, we regularly celebrate as a team. Learn from my shortcomings of the past: When you gather your leaders together to train them, take time to celebrate as well. Weave into your training specific times to stop and ask what people are learning. Celebrate those discoveries and tie them into how you as a church are living out the call to make disciples. This celebration leads to greater commitment and inspiration among your leaders, and it helps reinforce your culture. People will reproduce what you celebrate. So celebrate often! Let me share with you one more tip for celebrating at your training events: Ask disciple-makers to share wins from not only what they are learning but also their experiences discipling others. This looks like scheduling time for celebration when building your training agenda. Make sure to allow volunteers to share their celebrations so that everyone feels part of the win.

Living It Out

Remember when building your training event to plan—and even within the training itself—how you and your team can live out your cultural values. Think back to the relational way Jesus trained his disciple-makers. He taught the crowds, yes, but he implemented more focused training with his disciples. Sometimes this was just with Peter, James, and John, or with Mary, Martha, Lazarus, and a handful of others. Implement a training system where people can experience time to cultivate relationships, and make small groups the primary vehicle for teaching and giving information.

Think through the daily life of your church and ministry, your regular events, as well as *how you train*, and reimagine what it would look like to train people in a more intentional way. Use a relational small group format to train people whenever possible. When you train in a small group context like this, you are using the same relational model for your disciple-makers in which they will actually lead. As such, you are modeling for them the very format you are asking them to reproduce when they disciple others. This creates the necessary and consistent relational environment for the reproducible process to be effective.

Well-trained disciple-makers are essential to any biblical church that wants to accomplish the Great Commission of Jesus. When staff members and volunteers have all the training, skills, and knowledge they need, your church culture can be healthy. What's more, your church becomes attractive to the outside world. When this happens, take courage because your disciple-makers *can* storm up the hill of disciple-making, equipped and trained for what lies ahead. You are preparing an army on the verge of doing incredible things. The culture you have worked so hard to live out is becoming viral, and others are running right alongside you. They too are preparing to bring others along. At that point, my friends, you are a part of a movement that is reproducible.

12

MULTIPLY IT

Ensure your disciple-making culture is reproducible.

I rarely answer phone calls from numbers I do not know. One day, though, something stirred in me to answer a number I didn't know, and I am glad I answered. A man I will call Steve was on the other end. I remember the eager tone in his voice as he introduced himself and told me he was a church planter. With great enthusiasm he explained how passionate he was about his ministry, his new church, and how people were getting saved. He asked if he could buy me breakfast and get together to talk about "discipleship." Although I didn't have his number, he knew me from attending several conferences where I had spoken on the topic of disciple-making. Plus, he and his wife had planted their church two hours away from Houston, almost eight years prior.

As we talked on the phone, he said to me, "I have got to know the secret." He longed to know what we were doing that caused our church to grow from only four families to over 800 people in just three years. I told him I would help however I could by sharing our story. So we set a time to meet the following week at one of my favorite breakfast hang-outs.

At the restaurant, we found each other right away, and after a few pleasantries, he started firing questions at me about our curriculum, our staff structure, and the mechanics of how we lead small groups. He was dying to know what resource or strategy we had implemented that would unlock the secret to our church's growth. As you know by now, culture comes before strategy, but Steve wanted strategies without first looking at culture. In fact, understanding culture wasn't even on his radar.

Trying to find the right way to help him, I dodged most of his questions and tossed back to him a few basic answers about our small groups. Rarely pausing to take a breath, though, his enthusiasm spilled over, and tension began to build. The waitress came by to fill our cups of coffee and gave me a concerned look. It was like she could feel the tension too. But as the conversation carried on, I could sense something else happening, like he was avoiding an issue.

So I interrupted him and asked a question: "Steve, what does it mean to make a disciple of Jesus?" He sat there quietly while the waitress placed our food before us. Steve, still in silence, unfolded his napkin and began pushing his scrambled eggs around his plate.

I asked him, "Steve, are you okay?"

Steve looked up with frustration in his eyes. I could almost see the mental wrestling match going on in his head. Finally, he let out several long sighs and dropped his fork onto the plate with a loud clank, as if surrendering. Wringing his hands, his look now shifted from frustration to desperation, as he said, "Brandon, I have no idea how to make a disciple."

Now, I knew we were talking.

We dove into a long conversation about the culture Jesus created and how the change he wanted to see in his church must begin with his leaders. We discussed next steps and how he could be coached to be a disciple who makes disciples of Jesus.

I saw a spark in Steve's eye. He wanted to learn and change his ministry trajectory. Steve began talking with new hope, and even though all his questions were not answered that day, he at least had some direction. We talked about the Relational Discipleship Network, and how we coach churches. He began to understand that he too can create a culture where disciple-making is possible, and that culture can be multiplied throughout his church.

Remembering That Culture Is Who We Are

If you are going to make disciples and create a church culture where reproduction happens, you must take your cues from Jesus and embody disciple-making in your own life and ministry. Steve arrived at one of the important points we made earlier: to reproduce a disciple-making culture within our church, we must first *be it* before we can *multiply it.*

Jesus spent time talking about what it would require to be his disciple, but people picked up "what it looked like" primarily by being around him. A disciple would need to rearrange their priorities to make them fit within Jesus' kingdom priorities. Their own desires would have to take a backseat to the mission, and those desires may even need to die. The mission itself was best fleshed out in person so the first disciples could experience it, not just hear about it. Like what my friend Steve realized: In order to reproduce something, it must first become who we are. Only then can we intentionally pass it on to someone else. *This is foundational to a healthy culture of disciple-making.*

The truth that disciple-making must first become who we are was reinforced recently when I heard about a woman named Sharon who was just beginning her journey toward becoming a disciple-maker. She was preparing to lead her first small group of women,

Culture is
who we are.

and she was concerned that she didn't have the necessary skills to disciple them well.

Sharon's former small group leader, Ann, invited Sharon to accompany her on an errand one afternoon. While on this errand, Ann explained to Sharon that when you take someone with you, it provides an opportunity to spend time together and have deep conversation. Sharon's concerns about her disciple-making skills were relieved when she realized that she could easily invite a friend to spend an afternoon with her. When the time was right, Sharon decided to invest time with another lady named Teri, who was planning to attend her new small group. So just like her leader had done with her, she now invited this young mom to bring her two young kids on an errand—a shopping trip to Target. Sharon explained to Teri that with their kids in tow they could get their weekly shopping done together and connect with each other. Teri quickly responded, "Let's do it!"

That initial joint shopping trip turned into a weekly event for them. Whether at Target, the grocery store, or getting coffee at Starbucks, these two ladies made a habit of running errands together. This, along with meeting in weekly small group, helped their relationship blossom. They could now get errands done and have meaningful conversations along the way. They talked about friendships, work, and marriage, and they often discussed the truth of Scripture.

Just a few weeks into their weekly get-togethers, Teri expressed her gratitude to Sharon for the investment in her life. Teri was seeing its fruit in her walk with the Lord and in her family. What's more, she saw that it met a unique need in her life, and she even expressed a desire to help meet that need for other women too. What had been passed on to Sharon was now being passed on to Teri, and in a short time, Teri was already considering how to disciple others as well. That's "who we are" disciple-making culture.

Notice how their church's culture impacted their relationships. Let me point out several truths for you to grab ahold of as you process this for your context:

- Sharon had first been discipled by Ann and saw a model of what making disciples looks like.
- Sharon understood that disciple-making doesn't happen just in small groups.
- Sharon felt freedom to reach out and invite Teri.
- Sharon had been invested into by Ann, who gave her an opportunity to lead her own group.
- When Teri is ready, she will naturally start discipling others.

Sharon and Teri experienced the process of disciple-making in a way that changed both of their lives. The effect of that experience piqued a desire in both of them to create that experience for others.

That, friends, is the commission given by Jesus, and living into that commission is the process of seeing the Holy Spirit drawing people close to Jesus in a reproducible way. We build a culture where those who are being discipled know how to live out their calling to make disciples of Jesus Christ. People are intrigued by the idea of a disciple-making culture, but experiencing it for themselves is what really lights a fire in them to go and live it. Real-life disciple-making experience is not only the best teacher but it is also the best motivator. And that is why it must be who we are, not just what we do. New Testament disciple-making falls apart when we relegate it to a classroom. The culture of a church will become stale, even lifeless, if we do that. What Sharon and Teri experienced exuded life, and they grew as disciples by living out the culture Jesus so clearly modeled.

Be What You Want Others to Reproduce

Do you want to know what ended up happening with my pastor friend Steve? Let me tell you: He struggled because his understanding of the life of Christ was mostly academic; he needed to *experience* Jesus-style disciple-making. He knew what so many know "disciple-making" to be: a formalized class that transfers biblical information with little to no practical life application. In his twenty-four years of being a Christian, with seventeen of those years being in full-time ministry, he had never seen what biblical disciple-making looked like. Even during our breakfast meeting, he made an incredibly profound statement to me: "I cannot reproduce something I have no idea how to do!" We spent the rest of the breakfast unpacking what it would look like for him to begin the process of building healthy disciple-making culture, starting in his own life. Again, he knew that it must start with him! Steve went back to his church and started a small group, where he began discipling people. He learned he must *be something* before he could intentionally *reproduce something*.

How to Create a Reproducible Process

In order to create a disciple-making culture, you must solidify a process that's reproducible. Here are four principles to help you create a process that promotes reproduction:

1. Reproduce what you've successfully applied. As I've mentioned several times by now, you've got to experience this stuff first. If you don't know how to multiply disciples, then ask the Holy Spirit to teach you as you read the Gospels, pray, and put yourself out there to try. If you don't have the help of another person, ask God to provide that person. Learn how to make disciples on a small scale before you start teaching others.

2. Remember to keep it simple. For some reason, our natural bent as humans is to overcomplicate things. We design complex strategies to turn a process like disciple-making into something only those with a PhD in organizational systems can understand. But we know from Scripture that those first disciples of Jesus were just ordinary, untrained men.

3. Identify the key transitions. Look for the markers along the way that demonstrate growth in a budding disciple. For example, growth is evident when a person becomes more others-focused and less self-focused. Another transition happens when a disciple begins to step out and disciple someone for the first time. Identify key milestones that show the work of the Holy Spirit in their spiritual growth. In a book I co-authored, *Real-Life Discipleship Training Manual,* we created a tool called "The Discipleship Wheel," which you might find helpful in creating your own process.[6]

4. Understand the needs. Clearly defining what a person needs in order to grow will help you identify the "how to" of helping them progress as a disciple. Ask yourself, *Do they need more biblical training? Are they struggling to be relational with others in general?* When you understand their needs, only then can you help them mature. Just as Jesus understood what his disciples needed because of his close relationship with them, we too must be in close proximity to those we disciple so we can meet their needs and gently guide them along.

Keeping It Simple

Your reproducible process should be simple, and it should come out of the same process that Jesus modeled. His methods included great depth but also simplicity. Getting others to grasp the simplicity of disciple-making usually requires a lot of work. Years of programmatic thinking and curriculum-led ministry can cause deep ruts that are difficult to overcome. If I had a dollar for every time I have described what a disciple-making life looks like, only to hear someone to say in response, "It cannot be this simple," I could probably pay off my house. Okay, that's hyperbole, but you get the point. The process of disciple-making is as simple as imitating Jesus for others by sharing the gospel, sharing your day-to-day life, modeling healthy spiritual habits, walking with others through difficult circumstances, and expressing truth and love through it all.

At the time of writing this, our staff members and elders are currently working with a wonderful church-planting team in Arizona. Oftentimes in our discussions with their team, I explain the importance of keeping the process of disciple-making simple. Most people familiar with church culture think of disciple-making as more complicated than it is and, therefore, something they are not capable of cultivating. This feeds into many of their fears and insecurities about disciple-making. When we make it simple and keep it that way, we are able to address their hesitations and alleviate many of their concerns. Disciple-making may not be easy, but it can be simple. When we keep it simple, it becomes easily reproducible.

Jesus had a simple way of life that modeled what he intended for his disciples. He lived out spiritual disciplines in a way they could see with their own eyes. Jesus went beyond using words to demonstrate things like spending time alone with God, prayer, intentionality, love, friendship, humility, kindness, compassion, mercy, acceptance, grace, and forgiveness. He modeled these things with his life. He engaged his disciples by being with them, explaining things to them, challenging them, sending them, debriefing with them, teaching them, and praying with—and even for—them.

During leader training events, we often ask people to call out loud the characteristics of Jesus during his life on earth. The list inevitably includes most of the attributes and actions I mentioned in the previous paragraph. At the end of the exercise, we point to the list and ask attendees, "Can you do this? Can you love people like this? Can you be their friend? Can you walk with them through hard times? Can you point them to the Father?"

They begin to see the simplicity of Jesus' methods. They also begin to believe that they can make disciples. Disciple-making is more about transferring a Christ-centered lifestyle than transferring information. The process of disciple-making is not helping people know more about Jesus; it's helping them grow in the way of Jesus. It's not complicated; it's actually quite simple.

Every once in a while, songs on my smartphone music app will somehow end up in repeat mode rather than in shuffle mode. The same song plays over and over again. I don't usually notice it until the same song has played for the third or fourth time! While I find repeat mode annoying when it comes to my music, repetition is essential for multiplication. Church culture today often demands new and exciting entertainment. But Jesus was a fan of repeat mode, and we should be fans of it too. When making disciples is simple, we can keep those we lead on track through simple repetition and reinforcement. We point them back to the basic principles, remind them of the goal, and repeat the same basic maxims. While "Aha!" moments are good, "Oh, yeah!" moments are critical!

13

BUDGET FOR IT

*Invest time and resources into the
process you are cultivating.*

Jesus' powerful statement, "Where your treasure is, there your heart will be also," can help us understand more than just finances (Matt. 6:21). Like everything Jesus said, these words have profoundly impacted my approach to both life and ministry. Our true motives, desires, and even sometimes the selfish motives within us tell us exactly where our heart is.

Several years ago, I was coaching a large church that wanted to make changes and become more focused on disciple-making. Before we even began our discussion on the topic, I asked a question to all the leaders in the room: "Are you all sure you want to make this shift?" I often ask this question of other churches in their situation because I know they will have to make painful decisions that will require not just steps of faith, *but leaps of faith.*

The leaders at the table at this conversation in particular looked back at me and gave a unified "Yes!" They said they wanted to make the necessary shifts to be more obedient to God's call to make disciples. So we began to have the necessary hard talks to examine where in their large church they would have to start making changes. Little did they know that these types of discussions do not lead to a beautiful mountaintop experience (at least not immediately); they lead to a dimly-lit hallway that ends with a mirror—one that forces you to ask yourself a hard question, even beyond the "Are you sure?" question. The real question is this: "Are you willing to invest everything you have and all that you are into this process that Jesus gave so much of his life to?"

Making the Hard Choices

When Jesus made the statement about your treasure and your heart from Matthew 6 (mentioned above), he was holding up a mirror for self-reflection. So I propose to you a bit of self-examination in light of this. Ask yourself, *Am I willing to invest today for tomorrow's impact?* Look directly at the person in the mirror and ask, *Am I truly willing to invest into what it takes to build a healthy disciple-making culture? Do I really want this process that follows the model of Christ and pleases my king?*

> *Am I willing to invest today for tomorrow's impact?*

How you answer these questions will inevitably dictate where you will direct resources and how you will arrange your calendar. In our weekly staff meetings, we discuss how we are investing our time, efforts, and budget into disciple-making. We keep the conversation about the present and make sure it's relevant so that our hearts are aligned with the Great Commission to which Jesus calls us. Losing sight of this call can cause your church culture to shift or even radically change into something you never wanted or intended it to become.

During my third meeting with that large church I was coaching, they pulled out a huge spreadsheet to begin looking at where they were spending every dollar. Within minutes, I could hear the air go out of the room, and I could see shoulders sink and heads hang. I stopped the downward spiral that had begun and asked a question, "What is going on inside of each of you right now?"

The executive pastor looked up at me and said, "Our entire budget will need to change because over fifty percent of it goes toward the Sunday morning show." The senior pastor added, "We have hundreds of thousands of dollars going to missions organizations, and if I am being honest, we have no idea what is happening in those ministries. Are they making disciples? I have no idea."

We began to discuss where their annual budget was directed. The initial response by the group was to swing a pendulum and change everything. I strongly cautioned against such a swift response. Each area of their budget needed to be analyzed, and they had to be willing to make changes. To make these changes, there must be a strong dedication to prayer and following the Holy Spirit. The process of change needed to be intentional as well. As a group, they began a process of reducing what was spent on lights, cameras, and smoke machines (literally), and they started looking for other areas to change in their budget too. They wanted to find more areas where budget dollars could be moved to better invest into people. This was a true test of how sincerely they wanted to change the culture of their church.

Look in the Mirror

What about you? Have you decided to make the hard choice of truly investing into disciple-making? You must make that decision before you can truly create a reproducible disciple-making culture. Each decision-making leader in your church must understand there is more to our investment than just dollars and cents. To what are you dedicating your effort and energy in general? When I think of investing into a disciple-making culture so that it can become reproducible, several critical areas of investment come to mind: not just the financial areas of the church but also the strategy, staffing, leadership development—and even the younger generations—must all play into this type of planning. Below I have provided a list to help you prioritize your budget. I hope these examples will help you process what is appropriate for your context. I've divided them into "budgeting for disciple-making" in general and "hiring personnel for disciple-making" in particular.

Budgeting for Disciple-Making

In the earliest days of our church plant, our leadership team met in my family's living room and prayed as we began to discuss the budget. Several of the men whom I was developing as possible future elders helped me process what a budget formed around disciple-making might look like. We brainstormed together, and through prayerful consideration we began to whiteboard a budget strategy for staffing, facilities, programming, and investing into future leaders. This is a great exercise for any church who wants to budget for disciple-making. Here's some guidance from what we at Real Life Ministries Texas have learned, as you think through budgeting for your church in general:

Staff budgeting. In most churches, staffing generally comprises fifty percent of the budget. We wanted to go even higher because of our values, so our salary budget was set, and continues to remain, at around sixty percent. The money is not allocated toward higher salaries but toward more personnel. In fact, we agreed to sacrifice and keep our salaries on the lower end of the scale so that we can open up more opportunities to add additional staff as we grow. We began with, and continue to hire, the best disciple-makers in whom we see a calling to ministry.

During our first three years, we have intentionally hired people who have been discipled and are making disciples in our church

Budget for
disciple-making.

culture. Sometimes hiring from outside your church is necessary as well. A word of caution, though: interview thoroughly. Those not raised up in a disciple-making culture often struggle to make the transition.

Let me give you an example of raising up Aaron, our youth pastor, from within. He was raised up through our disciple-making culture and is one of the best disciple-makers I know. I would have no problem moving him to almost any position within the organization. Why? Because Aaron is a disciple-maker first and a youth pastor second, and countless hours have been spent investing into him so he can be the best disciple-maker he can be. He just happens to fit the role of youth pastor the best, but I am confident that all those under Aaron, in whatever area he might lead in our church, would grow spiritually within a healthy culture of biblical disciple-making. That's the power of a reproducible disciple-making process.

If you are creating a culture of disciple-making, you should develop, over time, a pipeline of future leaders. Investing into staffing is part of that future planning. I strongly encourage you—whatever role you play in church ministry—to help support, encourage, and develop a budget that places a high priority on investing into your strongest disciple-makers.

Facilities budget. Churches commonly set a goal of having twenty-five to thirty-three percent of their budget set aside for facilities, but that amount will tend to put pressure on other areas of your budget. Again, in our early discussions of planting, we focused on building strong disciples first, and, as we grew, we then looked toward finding facilities. So if you are planting a church, be mindful of building, rent, and remodel costs, not to mention other expenses. A heavy facility burden on your budget early on in a church can hinder your other long-term priorities. If you are in an existing church or ministry, find ways to cut your overhead facilities costs. Just as you might save with a home budget, look for ways to save and use the money in this category in more life-changing ways.

Unfortunately, in the Western church, buildings are a major part of the game. I have heard wonderful stories of house church movements around the world, but in today's culture, it can be difficult to create momentum without a central place to gather. I sometimes make the mistake of downplaying buildings so much that some people think I don't care about them at all. That is not true. I do care; I just want to ensure that we manage every dollar well and don't become extravagant. I have yet to meet a non-Christian who was losing their marriage, for example, and cared about how fancy our buildings look (or don't look). Prioritize disciple-making that saves marriages and budget for facilities in light of that.

Programming budget. When you are focused on disciple-making, then disciple-making becomes your filter for everything else. Walk with me back to that mirror we discussed above and ask yourself these questions:

- Does [*insert name of ministry program*] help us better make disciples? How do I know that?
- When people enter or leave [*insert name of ministry program*], what kind of spiritual growth do we see?
- How much money are we spending on [*insert name of ministry program*]? Can we see disciples being made there?
- On a scale from one to ten, how willing am I to make the financial changes that are necessary to see a disciple-making culture flourish in our church?

I encourage those who are making changes to an existing organization with this advice: *take your time transitioning budget allocations.* You are already working hard to change your culture, and as that shift occurs, budget adjustments need to happen, but they don't need to happen all at once. The larger the organization or ministry, the more slowly you will need to move. Think of your church as a boat: Small boats can make quick turns, but larger boats require more time and space to redirect them without causing unnecessary damage. Be wise in your assessment of whether you are turning a motorboat or a cruise ship.

Hiring Personnel for Disciple-Making

In the chapter "Train It" (above), I talked about the importance of training disciple-makers. Churches with an effective disciple-making culture train their people based on areas of their church that currently need attention. Much like setting a budget that is based on future plans, we must also look toward the future when investing into personnel. So allocate budget dollars that will support the hiring of staff that leads toward a disciple-making culture.

For example, I'm currently investing into a young man in my small group who is brand new to the Lord. He has almost no biblical background and is as green as they come. His passion to follow Jesus is strong, but he is still an infant in Christ. In the coming months, I plan to disciple him and give him small tasks to do. I am going to invest into him now, fully anticipating that God has great plans for him ahead of us. I will give him the opportunity to be faithful in a way that may seem small to you and me, but for him, it will be life-changing.

Let's return to the mirror for more self-reflection, once again, for the following questions which might call out a misplaced treasure you are holding onto. I encourage you to honestly ask yourself these questions:

- *To whom am I giving away small tasks today, fully planning on them either filling my current role or taking on other, larger roles in the future?*

- *What am I giving away today that will help develop at least one leader tomorrow?*
- *What core fear keeps me from giving away tasks to others?*

Those are hard questions to ask yourself. I personally sometimes struggle with a fear that I will "not get it right," or that I might miss something and coach a person in a wrong direction. I'm afraid that they will fail and I will be responsible for the failure. We are humans, and this process can bring out all kinds of fears.

I've found that many of us are afraid to train up leaders because they might get the credit for something we did or progress beyond us. If that's you, don't be afraid. Think about how Jesus modeled humility and having a servant's heart. He even told his disciples that they would do even greater things than he did (John 14:12–14). Obviously, he would never be surpassed as a leader, but their "takeover" of what he had started didn't threaten him at all. He demonstrated a servant's heart all along and invested into the future personnel who would lead his church. As he invested into his disciples, we must invest too.

So I ask this: In whom are you investing today who will later lead and disciple others? Are you planning for and aligning your budget dollars to better equip your people and align your church to live out a disciple-making culture? A lack of resources or investment can cause the movement to wither, instead of flourish. Remember, we are accountable to build *and develop*. While the physical buildings, equipment, and technology of Sunday morning services can be great and helpful tools, we are ultimately responsible for building up disciples into maturity. Establishing and maintaining alignment keeps things moving in the right direction.

Sample Budget Percentages for Disciple-Making Churches

I encourage you to download a document called "Budget Percentages for Disciple-Making Churches" at **himpublications.com/ culture.** This is a sample budget I created to help you budget for a reproducible disciple-making process. It will help you better align your budget to your disciple-making values. You could say that this will help you put your money where your culture is. Churches often talk about making disciples or even of the hope that one day they will see a culture of disciple-making that reproduces strong disciple-makers. Yet their budget reveals that cash flow sometimes feeds programs of little or no impact on the disciple-making process. That's why I wanted to offer this sample budget. Go to **himpublications.com/culture** and look for "Budget Percentages for Disciple-Making Churches." This will help you brainstorm ideas on how to make financial adjustments to your budget.

14

ALIGN IT

*Pull everything together toward a
healthy disciple-making culture.*

As a young teenager, I had a summer job working for my grandparents on their little farm in Northern Idaho, where I learned about the importance of alignment. My job was to change the location of the sprinkler pipes that irrigated the pasture. The summers in Idaho can be brutally hot and dry. On multiple occasions, I needed to move the sprinkler pipes more than once a day!

Now to give all the non-farmers context, let me explain: The sprinkler pipes on their farm were aluminum, four inches in diameter and approximately twenty feet long, with a large sprinkler head at one end. These pipes were connected together end-to-end and running across the length of the pasture. The first pipe of the line was attached to a large valve on the main water line. At the far end of the stretch, the pipes were capped. This massive line of pipe needed to be moved on a daily basis so that the entire field could be watered during the course of a week.

What does all this have to do with disciple-making alignment? Well, one of the most critical parts of this job on the farm was to lay the pipe *in a straight line*. We had markers on the fencing so that when you began to lay the first few pipes in a line, you could aim for those markers to keep the pipes straight. If the pipes were not in a straight line, not only did it look terrible, but water never reached some parts of the field, causing parched, dry spots to appear. The pipes *had to be aligned*. I will admit that some early mornings—half awake and frankly not always paying attention—I looked down my line and realized it more closely resembled a huge silver snake working its way through the pasture than it did a line of sprinkler pipes. On those days, I had to go back and reset the misaligned sections. If I did not make the corrections early in the job, the rest of the line would be a mess.

Jesus Prayed for Alignment

Cultural alignment is a concept that affects families, businesses, teams, and even churches. I believe the devil will fight to disrupt alignment more than anything else in your life and your church. I previously mentioned Jesus' prayer in John 17, and as we come to a close, let's read this prayer again, focusing on the alignment language:

> My prayer is not for them alone. I pray also for those who will believe in me through their message, *that all of them may be one*, Father, just as you are in me and I am in you. May they also be in us so that the world may believe that you have sent me. I have given them the glory that you gave me, *that they may be one as we are one:* I in them and you in me. *May they may be brought to complete unity* to let the world know that you sent me and have loved them even as you have loved me. (John 17:20–23)

Jesus prayed for us to be unified—that is, to be relationally aligned with him and with each other. According to Jesus, nothing is more effective and powerful than his body living in alignment. Our physical bodies function more healthfully when all of our systems are in alignment, and the same is true for the church. When the physical body gets out of alignment, it can get diseases more easily or even die. Again, the same is true of our churches. Jesus could have prayed for so many other things, but he prayed for one central thing: unity.

Remember the sprinkler pipes again: if I lost focus on keeping one pipe aligned with the next, the whole line would stray, resulting in a dry, unhealthy pasture. That's how it is with our world too: When we succumb to society's gravitational pull toward chaos and disunity, we fail to accomplish anything worthwhile. This comes from our sinful nature, which draws us away from the truth of God. The society we live in will always pull us toward discord, misalignment, and affliction. We must resist this and learn to seek the unity of God in Christ.

I often say that keeping any group of people moving in one direction, aligned and together, is like trying to load monkeys onto a flatbed truck: If you throw ten in the bed of the truck, three immediately jump off, two start swinging from the tailpipe, and several others run to the front and try to drive. In any organization, including the church, keeping people aligned is hard work.

How to Keep Everyone Aligned

So how do we accomplish this? How do we keep this group of people called "the church" together? I have listed several critical elements below, which our church has carefully held to over the last few years. I have observed these same guiding principles in existing churches who have successfully made the shift to being strong disciple-making churches. As we near the end of this book, let me share with you four guiding principles to help you align your church's disciple-making culture:

1. Fight encroachment. Over a period of years (before we moved to Houston), my wife and I cultivated a huge vegetable garden. We carved out a big section on our property and created an ideal spot to grow all kinds of fruits and vegetables. I remember the back-breaking work of tilling the existing soil and adding to it different nutrients the soil needed. We removed rocks, tore out weeds, and eventually got the ground ready for us to plant a healthy garden. Every week, I would walk around the garden and notice where the weeds, grass, and other native plants were encroaching back into the garden. The natural world around my garden wanted to take this land back. On a daily basis, Amber and I had a fight these intruders on our hands and knees to keep the garden healthy.

Not only do you need to fight spiritual encroachment in the church and in your home, but you also, and most importantly, need to fight it in your own life. In Matthew 13, Jesus warns us of the perils of thorns and weeds among healthy plants in "The Parable of the Sower" and "The Parable of the Weeds." We must keep the weeds out of our lives and fight for a healthy culture. To remove them, we must first identify them. So search for and expect stealthy, yet invasive, weeds that crop into your disciple-making culture.

I remember one day during a staff meeting, one of our team members mentioned that a new small group leader wanted to start another small group using a very controversial curriculum (one I knew to be divisive in nature). The leader who wanted to begin this group was not equipped to deal with the problems I knew might creep in. Innocently, this person wanted to go off and do their own thing, not realizing that what they were planning to use could cause disunity within our culture.

A weed was sprouting, so I asked our team, "What do you think we should do?" After we discussed it, our team landed on a solid, clear, and loving plan to walk through the issue. They did an excellent job executing the plan too, and the volunteer felt loved and is leading an effective small group today. The volunteer stayed in our church, but the "weed" in the garden was removed.

This sort of gardening is different than the pruning we talked about above. I would call this "weeding." In gardening terms, pruning is removing the unproductive or diseased parts of a plant to increase its fruit; weeding is removing other intrusive plants which sprout up and threaten to choke out the healthy plant. In church, pruning refers to removing or scaling back programs or ministries which are not producing disciples; weeding refers to resolving issues which could invade and hinder disciple-making in otherwise healthy ministries. In short, weeding protects the culture and ensures that your church remains aligned. When our staff walked the new small group leader through the potential disunity that might come from their proposed curriculum, they were doing some weeding, thereby avoiding future problems by removing small issues that were sprouting.

Removing the weeds that threaten your culture requires hard work. Plus, a bit of experience helps you know what is a healthy, fruit-producing plant that should stay and what is a weed. You have to become an experienced gardener, you could say, to know how to quickly spot the threats. Yes, fighting encroachment is hard work that requires diligence and a keen eye, which is important to know. But most importantly, keep in mind that *you cannot do this on your own!* You must rely on the Holy Spirit to guide you and give you the necessary discernment to remain aligned as a team and to fight those nasty little weeds that creep in, causing disunity and distracting you from disciple-making. Unless this happens, church culture becomes unhealthy.

2. Be empowered by the Holy Spirit. We certainly must do our part to maintain alignment in our churches. Yet we also must remember this whole thing—church, disciple-making, and the Great Commission—*is God's idea*. The church belongs to Jesus, and without the power of the Holy Spirit, we are dead in the water. Trying to cultivate a church culture without the Holy Spirit yields no fruit; that is like trying to cultivate a garden without sunlight. The power we receive from the Holy Spirit might be the most critical part in the entire process of cultivating a disciple-making culture.

I tend to rely on myself to get things done. I rely on the Holy Spirit for a little while, then I tend to drift and find myself fairly independent once again. In God's loving kindness, he gently reminds me of how I have drifted. In order to keep our church aligned and going in one direction, I must constantly abide in Christ. You and I are both dependent on him to fill us, show us, and teach us what we need in order to have a healthy culture where effective disciple-making can take place.

3. Inspect the fruit. Within every organization, good leadership inspects and evaluates outcomes. Leaders ask of the organization, "Are we successfully producing what we actually want to produce?"

When Amber and I planted our first vegetable garden, we fully anticipated that each plant would produce a bumper crop. Some plants shot up and produced well, but others not so much. On a daily basis, we walked through the garden and looked at each plant. Sometimes a plant required more water than at other times, or it needed additional nutrients in order to thrive. We knew this because we were regularly inspecting the fruit. That's what disciple-making leaders do too.

In John 15, we read that Christ is the vine, the Father is the gardener, and we are the branches. We also know from this passage that Jesus expects us to bear fruit: "This is to my Father's glory, that you bear much fruit, showing yourselves to be my disciples" (v. 8). When I talk about inspecting fruit, I'm simply saying that we look for the results of God's work in a person's life, and in the church as well, which we can see in practical ways.

I've had many conversations with Christians about the spiritual fruit of their lives. Likewise, I have talked with pastors about the fruit of their churches. Almost one hundred percent of the time I ask a pastor about how their church is doing, the main measurement of success (or "fruit") they mention is Sunday morning attendance. Sunday morning metrics can certainly be an indicator of what is going on in the church, but I believe this indicator can easily be deceiving. *The most important fruit to inspect is how well aligned are a church's disciple-making efforts.* You can inspect disciple-making fruit by asking questions like the following about whether people are growing spiritually: Are most of your adults regularly participating in disciple-making small groups? Are your small groups growing and branching? Are more and more people serving in your church? Are you hearing stories of changed lives?

When our churches are not committed to a unified goal of effective disciple-making, we become misaligned and drastically limit our ability to produce the bountiful fruit of disciple-making. Have the courage to go and inspect fruit, and have even more courage for hard conversations about aligning ministry goals, staff, and volunteer development, not to mention how well church resources are producing disciples rather than mere attendees, or even converts.

4. Celebrate the wins. In several other places in this book, I have mentioned the importance of celebration. I remember the mental high fives I gave myself after the long, hard work of laying those pipes straight in the field, turning on the water, and effectively watering the pasture. Beautiful fruit includes changing lives, souls committed to Christ's mission, and people stepping up for the first time to be discipled and to disciple someone else. As disciple-makers we *must* celebrate the bountiful harvest. When we celebrate disciple-making, we clarify the goals of our culture, which solidifies organizational alignment.

At our church, we have used all forms of technology to capture stories and share them with the whole body of our church. Sunday services, social media, and other gatherings can offer great venues for celebration. We gather regularly just to celebrate what God is doing in our midst. Ministry is hard work and keeping everyone aligned can drain the most dedicated of Christians. Celebration helps us remember why we are doing what we are doing, and the church will aspire to reproduce what we are excited about.

We all, as disciples of Jesus, have been given a commission. Together, as the collective body of Christ, we are to be disciples who pursue disciple-making. We owe everything to Jesus. We must emulate the culture he created and align ourselves with his Word and his Spirit. You and I must do our part to cultivate a disciple-making culture.

CONCLUSION

Let's Get to Work!

I often find myself wondering if I have been successful at accomplishing what Jesus has called us to do. I am sure you sometimes wrestle with this question too. Hopefully throughout this book, you have gained key knowledge that will help you get to work building or changing toward becoming a church with a healthy disciple-making culture. For me, when I doubt anything on this journey, I lean on the Lord and go back to what works. In this book, we have established how the key components of a disciple-making culture work. These are the headings of each major section of this book: Biblical Foundation, Intentional Leadership, Relational Environment, and Reproducible Process.

Now, at the end of this book, I want to go back to these with you to exhort and encourage you with them. I also want to add some final thoughts about my journey of creating a disciple-making culture under each of these headings:

Key Component 1: Biblical Foundation. The Bible is our plumb line, and the Gospels give us a beautiful picture of what it looks like to be a disciple who makes disciples. When doubt creeps in or you wonder what to do next, remember to start with the Scriptures. Examine especially those fine details that surround the life of Christ. Remember that Jesus is the greatest disciple-maker to have ever walked the earth, and his methods are always best. Stop and examine your life, your ministry, and your church to make sure you are following Jesus' model of disciple-making as best you can.

Key Component 2: Intentional Leadership. I sometimes wonder if I am making a difference to truly impact lives. If this doubt enters your mind, take my advice and ask yourself, *How am I doing at being intentional? Am I holding true to what I am communicating? Are there ministry areas in our church that need to be pruned?* A healthy disciple-making culture requires leaders who are focused and intentionally living out the values that uphold the culture.

Key Component 3: Relational Environment. Fulfilling the Great Commission is not for the faint of heart; it takes dedication to nurture relationships that help toward that end. Remember that these relational environments carry the culture of disciple-making, which means they are vital for cultivating this culture. We know Jesus modeled healthy relationships and commanded us to love God and each other—which can only happen in life-on-life relationships.

Key Component 4: Reproducible Process. When it comes to building a disciple-making culture, there is no greater joy than witnessing others replicate what you've modeled. Sometimes, after I have spent countless hours investing into someone, I am challenged by the fact that the time to release them has come. I am reminded that I am working in God's kingdom, not mine. If you struggle with this at any point, remember that unless you see the process of disciple-making go beyond yourself, you really have not made disciples who can make disciples. When that does happen, though, celebrate!

Let's Do This

No matter where you are on the journey or what lies ahead of you, remember that you can do this! Whether planting a church or transitioning an existing church, God will do the work in you, with you, and through you. I know he wants to use you to ignite a fire for disciple-making, born in a culture that reflects New Testament truth. I know you can do this because it is the will of God that you do. The Holy Spirit will do this work in you and through you as you're guided by the Holy Scriptures.

Each part of this book touches on a different aspect of cultivating a disciple-making culture. I am thankful that the Lord has allowed me to experience this type of culture. I can see the fruit, and I know that fulfilling the Great Commission is not just some lofty goal from the New Testament era. The culture they lived out back then and we seek to live out now, by the power of the Holy Spirit, can translate into the vital lifeblood of our churches. It really is possible! I've experienced it time and time again, and I challenge you to go live it out too.

Take the principles I've provided for you here, dive deep into the Scriptures, and go create healthy culture. Be a disciple-maker right where God has planted you. Allow your disciple-making to be like that of the disciples we read about in the early church. You and I are here today to pursue what it means to accomplish the Great Commission because it is *who we are*, not just *what we do*. Let's get to work. Let's go cultivate disciple-making churches.

Where to Go from Here?

To finish, I want to provide some clear next steps you can take to begin shifting your church culture. I know some points along the way may have left you wondering where you can get some help. So I suggest three steps you can take:

1. Start living it. The most important next step, and I hope you already have started thinking this way, is to start living out all that we have covered in this book.

2. Attend a discipleship conference like those offered by Discipleship.org. These events put you around other like-minded disciple-makers so you can learn with others who are in a similar pursuit of Jesus and the Great Commission.

3. Pursue coaching. The Relational Discipleship Network, for which I serve as a board member, coaches churches and ministries to make the culture shifts they are trying to make. You can learn more about what we do and sign up for our next DiscipleShift 1 training by going to rdn1.com. From that site, you can also request to be coached by one of our network coaches.

NOTES

1. *The Discipleship Gospel* (Nashville: HIM Publications, 2018).

2. *The Discipleship Gospel*, 31.

3. *Stay the Course* (Nashville: HIM Publications, 2017). Visit www.himpublications.com to find out more about this book.

4. To learn more, visit rdn1.com.

5. See rdn1.com to learn more about the Relational Discipleship Network.

6. *Real-Life Discipleship Training Manual* by William S. Krause, William James Putman, Avery T. Willis Jr., and Brandon Guindon (Colorado Springs: NavPress, 2010), 111.

ABOUT THE AUTHOR

BRANDON GUINDON is the lead pastor of Real Life Ministries Texas. Brandon holds a master's degree in church leadership and New Testament theology from Hope International University. Ordained at Real Life Ministries in Post Falls, Idaho, he is the author of *Stay the Course*, is a co-author of *Real-Life Discipleship Training Manual*, and serves on the board of directors of the Relational Discipleship Network.

STAY
the
COURSE

Seven Essential Practices for
Disciple Making Churches

A **DISCIPLESHIP.ORG** RESOURCE

BRANDON GUINDON
foreword by JIM PUTMAN

A BOOK ABOUT

Seven Essential Practices for Disciple-Making Churches

"Well-defined guardrails to keep your church on the road of disciple-making."

—JIM PUTMAN

"*Stay the Course* is a great resource for identifying practical ways to make disciples in your church."

—BOBBY HARRINGTON

UTILIZE THIS SHORT RESOURCE TO HELP YOUR TEAM STAY ON THE DISCIPLE-MAKING TRACK

★ Equip your leaders to practice the essentials
★ Discuss best practices with your team
★ Engage Scripture along the way

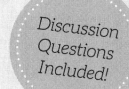

Discussion Questions Included!

ORDER THROUGH

www.himpublications.com

Made in the USA
Las Vegas, NV
20 October 2022